KUHKOMOSSONUK AKONUTOMUWINOKOT

Stories Our Grandmothers Told Us

KUHKOMOSSONUK AKONUTOMUWINOKOT

Stories Our Grandmothers Told Us

Edited by
Wayne A. Newell

Associate Editor
Robert M. Leavitt

Resolute Bear Press
Robbinston, Maine

Resolute Bear Press, Robbinston 04671

Printed in the United States of America

2 3 4 5 6 7 8 9

ISBN: 978-0-9988195-7-0

Illustrations:
Maliyan
Carole Thomayer

Passamaquoddy Stories 20th Century:
Roger Gabriel, *Kehtaqs-Ghost Stories, Ehpit naka Puwin-The Woman and the Corpse*
Robert M. Leavitt, *Amucalu-The Fly*
Faye Hoban, *Mahtoqehs naka Malsom-Hare and Wolf, Akonutomuwin-Tell Me A Story, Wahant-Devil Stories*

Peskotomuhkati Atkuhkakonol—Passamaquoddy Stories 19th Century:
Lee Suta

Thank you to Donald Soctomah of the Passamaquoddy Historic Preservation Committee for the cover photograph of Alice Sockabasin.

Book Design:
Valerie Lawson

Special thanks to the Passamaquoddy Tribe at Motahkomikuk and Sipayik.

Dedicated to Passamaquoddy storytellers,
who maintain our traditions from generation to generation

Introduction

Wayne A. Newell

The traditional Passamaquoddy stories in this volume create a bridge between the knowledge and memories of elders—my generation—and the world of today's younger people. Connections between the generations have been weakened over the past few decades with the potential loss of the Passamaquoddy language, although it is still spoken fluently by elders of the community. These stories help us understand how our community and culture have changed over the years and have come to be the way they are today.

Until just a few decades ago, these stories were told as an integral part of our Passamaquoddy home life. Since the late 1800s, thanks to intense interest in documenting the language and in ensuring its survival, many stories have been written down by native speakers or recorded by them on everything from Jesse Walter Fewkes's wax cylinders in the 1890s, the very first audio recordings of Native Americans, to contemporary analog and digital media. Despite the enormous changes seen over the past century, today's young people may still find speakers of Passamaquoddy who are able to share stories and the language in them.

Passamaquoddy stories were told in homes without the benefit of electricity or books. In my childhood, not having electricity enhanced storytelling. Shadows, cast by the flame of an oil lamp or a candle, created a kind of theatrical backdrop. Lying there listening, I watched the shadows moving on the ceiling. They were a significant factor in keeping my focus. There were few distractions. We children were respectful and quiet.

Between stories, the storyteller left time for discussion and for us to share our own experiences. She might talk about lessons, like the notion of respect. *Nomiyot wen, musa cikawiyahkoc* (if you see someone, don't make fun of them), my grandmother told us. In stories, people who mocked others or went to forbidden places might die prematurely or suffer an accident. One time I disobeyed and was picking beach peas on the shore, which I had been told not to do. My leg got badly cut. We learned these lessons as truths because of the environment in which the stories were told.

Storytelling was not a formal occasion. It might happen after supper, all of the grandchildren climbing into grandmother's bed at night and listening together as a group, hanging on her words, watching her face and gestures—and each other's—laughing at the well-deserved comeuppance of this person and shivering at the terrifying experience of another. Many were about people my grandmother had known. It was very different from watching television today, each of us in our own little space, watching people we will never meet in places we may never know. We learned that the people in the stories were real. My grandmother had once seen a wonakomehsis, a little person, from a distance. She told us, "When they're going to get married you'll hear them drumming in the rocks." My cousin and I went to listen for them.

Listeners regarded the stories they heard as magical, and the storyteller was in effect a channel between the people and events of that magical world and those who were listening. The teller laughed or commented on what was happening, as if the story had a life of its own, and all the people in the room were hearing it together.

Like all people, Passamaquoddy children and adults loved listening to the same stories over and over again. Storytellers were revered for their special knowledge and language skills. Few people in the communities had cars or bicycles, so we walked to a storyteller's house. We exchanged cigarettes or pipe tobacco for stories. She was grateful for the gifts and was happy to share the stories she had been told. Sometimes her house was full of children and adults who had come there just to listen.

Stories like those about Wahant (the Devil) were told to educate more than to frighten. They made children aware that the world wasn't all peaches and cream, that there were other forces in the world. We learned to be moderate in our behavior and to look beyond appearances. The handsome or well-dressed stranger might not be what he seemed. In fact, the Devil came to Pleasant Point. We could see where he had dragged a chain across a big rock.

Georgie Big John Soctomah, an elder who helped us recover the nineteenth-century language of the Koluskap stories found here, was the first to have a radio (battery-powered) at Indian Township. He noticed his family marveling as they listened. "How can it be that someone in Boston is talking right here?" In those days of the first radio sets, people gathered around to listen to a particular program, like listening to a storyteller. It was also one of the first opportunities to learn English outside of school. This began a change in the storytelling tradition. No longer did we know the people who were talking, and we got distracted by the novel technology. It was the mysterious stranger, some thought: *"Cu-al-lu wahant nit lamiw 'tihin"* (it must be the Devil in there). In a way, the sense of there being another world in stories transferred naturally to that strange voice coming through the air. Later, with television, the focus shifted to the picture, somehow even more remote than radio from our everyday oral traditions.

THE FIRST STORY IN THIS BOOK, "Maliyan," tells how my parents and grandparents grew up in the early 1900s. It shows how important stories were in children's upbringing. It was created from the memories of elders about their own childhoods, collected in the 1970s by Mary Ellen (Stevens) Socobasin. We learn what people's houses were like: houses without the modern conveniences, blankets hung up as partitions for privacy, no electricity or telephones. My mother told me about her childhood laundry days—several trips to the community well for next day's wash, putting the water to heat overnight on the stove. "Maliyan" reveals our standard of living and how the first changes from outside came into the community.

The stories that follow "Maliyan" are typical of those that a young girl's grandmother and aunt would have told her about animals, people in the community, the Devil, and ghosts. All of these had evolved naturally over the years from earlier, "classical" Passamaquoddy stories about Koluskap.

At the same time, our cultural outlook was gradually changing, developing along with our day-to-day experiences. Stories have always included our own daily activities— playing ball or cards, going to church, raising children, gardening, attending wakes. As our world changed, the stories took on new elements. The evil Pukcinsqehs gathered bird's eggs on an island in an older story. Espons made mischief with impatient people and became the Devil inciting jealousy or trying to one-up a gardener in more modern times.

Those older Passamaquoddy stories, the "Peskotomuhkati Atkuhkakonol" found in the final section of this book, were told orally for hundreds of years, and as late as the 1920s. My great-grandfather, Lewis Mitchell at Pleasant Point, wrote them down in Passamaquoddy in the 1880s to preserve them for future generations. They are Mitchell's own versions of legends common to all the eastern Algonquian languages. Like the more modern stories, they also teach lessons of moderation, respect, and proper behavior.

THE LANGUAGE IN THE STORIES exemplifies the eloquence of storytellers, the gifted speakers of their time, and the richness of spoken Passamaquoddy. As in other Algonquian languages, words are formed by combining a number of meaningful roots, so that speakers regularly invent new words to express precise meanings as they speak.

For example, in the story of "Mahtoqehs naka Malsom," *etoli-tomahqaluwehtuhuki*, 'when I got my tail cut off'—not a word heard in ordinary conversation—combines roots meaning 'separating,' 'stick-like,' 'tail,' 'chop,' and 'me.' As another example, in the story of Espons, *wapalokiqewocossultuwok*, 'the little ones eyes turned white with the cold,' puts together the meanings 'white,' 'eye,' 'be cold,' 'little,' and 'they.' This word not only describes what happened to the the children but also, through the use of the diminutive (*oss*), expresses compassion for them. Storytellers were the consummate inventors of such words. Sometimes their inventions were playful, as when the uncle hands Sikiliyem's son an *amucaluwewi-wawikon* (a fly's backbone); with its alliterative syllables, we-wi-wa-wi, even the word itself sounds funny.

The bilingual text gives readers an opportunity to appreciate the language of Passamaquoddy storytelling and to understand how the language creates another, parallel world. Most of the English translations correspond sentence by sentence and paragraph by paragraph with the Passamaquoddy originals. In "Maliyan" the translation is freer, a version of the story as it would be told in English. It corresponds closely to the Passamaquoddy but differs in a few places, and therefore the text is organized chapter by chapter.

Contents

MALIYAN

MARY ANN

by

Mary Ellen Stevens Socobasin

Indian Township, Maine

1979

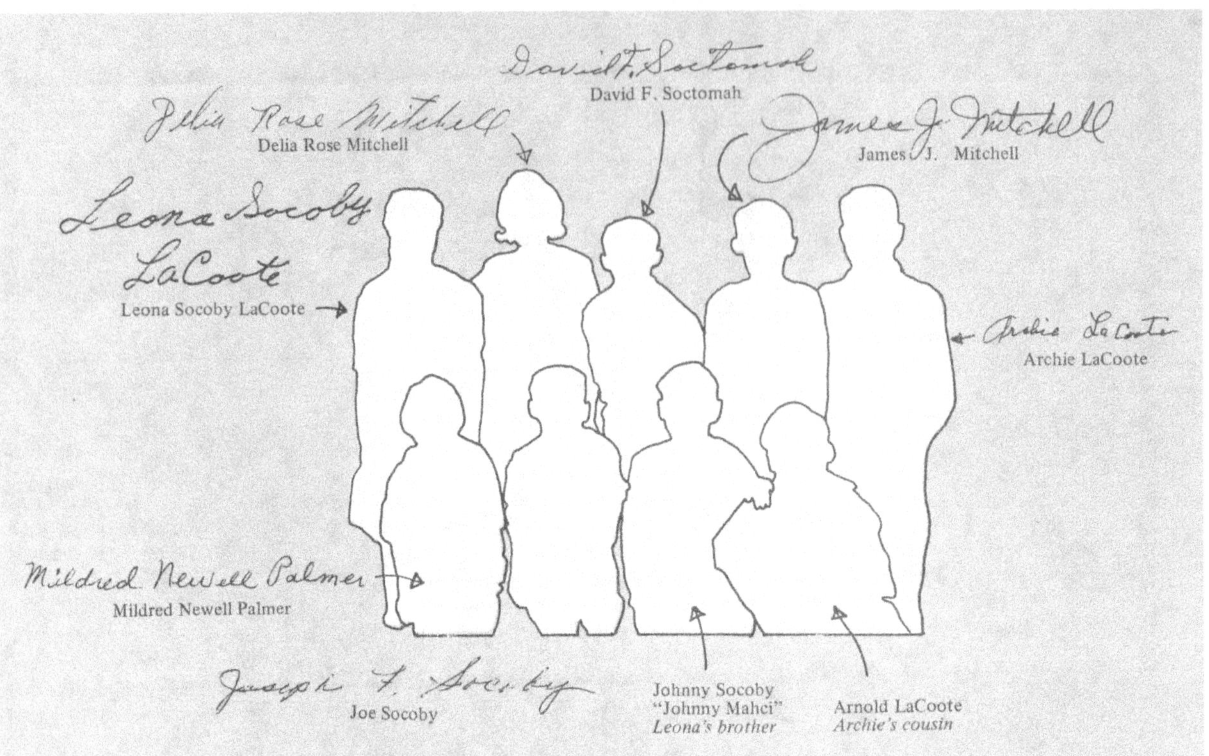

Yukk nit kisi-wicuhkeminokot weci-kisihtuwek yut wikhikon.
These people helped us make this book:

George Bailey
Adelaide Newell
Josephine Bailey
Elizabeth Newell
Lena Brooks
Fannie Newell
Albert Dana
Irene Newell
Joan Dana
Lizzie Newell
Louis Dana
Wayne Newell
Maria Dana
Joseph Nicholas
Philomene Dana
Peter Paul
Marion Davis
Lola Sockabasin
David Francis, Sr.
David Soctomah
Marion Francis
Arthur Sopiel
Lillian Gabriel
George Stevens, Jr.
Simon Gabriel
Seraphim Stevens
Anna Harnois
Sue Stevens
Archie LaCoote
Fred Tomah
Leona LaCoote
Maxine Tomah
Delia Mitchell
Newell Tomah
Eva Moulton
Virginia Wiseman

Originally written in Passamaquoddy by Mary Ellen Stevens Socobasin.
English version by Mary Ellen Stevens Socobasin and Robert M. Leavitt.

Edited by Wayne A. Newell

Photo layout and captions by Carol Thomayer.
Photo: "At School on the Strip"

1

Neqt yaq wot skicinuwi-pilsqehsis wiku utenek—liwisu Maliyan—wiciw wikuwossol, mihtaqsol, naka mossisol. Mossisol yaq kis kiskatomul; liwisu yaq Anuwit.

In the 1920's there was a little girl named Mary Ann living on the Strip at Indian Township. Also in the household were her mother and father and her older sister, Anna, as well as Anna's husband, Sabattus.

Elkihqahk wikuwawa. Ktomakte tahk, tehpu eli-wissektahasik pilasq, naka ma-te lamikuwam tomasokahasiw. Tan etuci yaq wen koti-atsewet, 'tahcuwi yaq wen ekhutun petqil cayisok. Nit-te eli-ksahayin, yut yaq-ote ehtek papskot, tuwihput, kutoputiyil. Waht yaq-ona oloqiw, kuhutiyil naka tuwiskut. Ipa, yut nit Maliyan wikit, nekom yaq-ote peyemi-wasisuwit. On-ote newonul kotokil wikuwamol nit eyikil.

Although the house was quite big, it was in poor condition. Outside, the walls were covered with roofing paper and narrow strips of wood. On the inside, they were covered with newspaper, and there were no partitions to separate one area of the house from another. If you wanted to change your clothes, you had to hang a quilt or a blanket from a rafter. In one corner, near the stove, were a table and chairs; on the other side, the beds and a chamber pot—because of course there is no bathroom indoors. This is where Mary Ann lives, and she is the youngest in the family. There are only four other houses nearby.

Ukomolcin yaka Maliyan etuceyit, on yaka kisihtasu ihtolokehkitimok. Ipa, on mace-kehkiman Maliyan naka witapihi. Eci yaq wikuwatokehkimut wasisok. Tomk-otehc ekehkimut elokisultihtit, tpaskutikonok, naka elintuhtihtit. Nutokehkikemit yaq wenuhcisqehs, 'cey utenek. Liwisu Mossos Welinton. Nit-tehc yaq Maliyan metokehkimut, macahan wikuwak, naciyan 'tamsqocehkanol weci-kisayyat.

When Mary Ann is eight years old, a schoolhouse is built. She and her friends can go to school now. They enjoy learning to read, to use numbers, and to sing. Mrs. Wellington, the children's teacher, is a white woman from the town of Princeton.

Peciyat wikuwak, wot tahk yaq wikuwossol weckuwi-posonutehkelit. Kis yaq newonul kisihtaqil, on-oc sepawonu natankuwehtun ikolisomanihkuk. Nit-oc yaq weci-kisonuhmuhtit nukhomon.

As soon as the school day is over, Mary Ann goes home to make a doll to play with. She finds her mother making baskets. Four completed baskets stand on the table ready to be sold in town tomorrow, so that they can buy flour.

Mihtaqsol yaq pahkak motekpehtihike. Mossisol yaq-ona kis toli-wolaqahqe. Nit ehtate Maliyan macekhahsin ahtulhawekonisol weci-kisiyat 'tamsqocehkanol, mesq welaqihpultihtihq. Tomk-ote yaq woniyakon kisihtuwat, 'siskul, wihton, apc 'tun. On yaka 'pihtinol, hok, 'qatol. Ipa, Tokkiw nihtol kisiyat, kis mossisol kisi-apuwisawe.

Etucihpultihtit, cuwi yaq Maliyan kossicuwenike, 'sami Anuwit 'tahcuwi-liqahsuwewal uskitapemol. Wikuwossol yaq-ona 'tahcuwi-wolatokuhutunol suwitokolasol.

Ipa, tan etuci 'kihka-kiseyultihtit, nit-tehc wikuwossol 'tuhpotun possaqhenomakon naka 'posqolenomon. Nit-tehc ulopin 'tolapekessutik, cel yuhtol utomakonol, naka 'tacomin mecimiw eleyikpon. Tan etuci mace-skuhumat wahantuwol, ecihc Maliyan cipomolsit.

Tan etuci yaq wikuwossol mehtacomilit, nit-tehc yaq ulaqaniya. Maliyan naka wikuwossol wihpetuwok 'sami ma tepiyewiyil kuhutiyil. Mihtaqsol-olu yaq pemsokhasik tolonekosu. Anuwit naka Sapatis waht yaq kikociw ote 'kuhutiwa. Keka yaq Anuwit nicaniw.

From the back of the house, Mary Ann hears the sound of her father pounding a stick of ash. There'll always be a good supply for making new baskets to sell so the family can have flour and other things they have to buy.

Anna is cooking supper. Before they sit down to eat, Mary Ann looks around for odd bits of rag to make herself a doll. By tying the rags together, she makes first the head—with eyes, nose and mouth made of buttons—then the arms, the body and the legs. By the time she is finished with her doll, supper is all ready—a delicious meal of potatoes and tumahsis, hot fry-bread made in a skillet.

Mary Ann washes the dishes. Anna is mending Sabattus's clothes, and their mother is busy coiling up a long braid of sweetgrass, back and forth, back and forth, in a neat figure 8.

As they work, the light grows dimmer in the house. Mary Ann's mother fills the lamp and lights it. Rocking gently in her rocking chair and smoking her pipe, she starts to talk about the things that happened a long time ago. Sometimes she tells stories about the Devil and how he came to different people. Then Mary Ann has an eerie feeling, and she moves a little closer to Anna and her mother. They go right to bed when the stories are over.

There aren't enough beds for everybody, so Mary Ann and her mother sleep together while her father makes a bed on the floor. Anna and Sabattus have their bed in another corner of the room. Their baby will be born any day now.

2

Spasuwiw amihkit Maliyan, kis-oc yaq eci-wolopotek. Kis yaq wikuwossol kistutuwe. Mihtaqsol-ona kis tolapilom. Tumahsis-ona kis tolaqosu, eli-spasihpultihtit. Nit-te yaq kisihpultihtit, Sapatis 'tolomi-natoluhkan, kcihkuk yaq tolluhke.

Before Mary Ann wakes up in the morning, her mother has made a fire in the stove and is cooking tumahsis in the iron skillet. The warm air and the familiar smell of the fry-bread have filled the house when Mary Ann opens her eyes. Her father comes in with water from the lake. After breakfast, Sabattus goes off to work in the woods, and Mary Ann has to go to school.

Maliyan yaq-ona cuwi-natokehkiman. Peciyat ihtolokehkitimok, kis yaq elinaqsit wasisok qocomok. Nit yaq-ote-na mote-suwahqihikan Mossos Welinton. 'Tolomi-ksiyatokominiya. Nit yaq-ote-na mace-kehkitin, tokkiw pasqekil. On-oc 'tahcuwi-maciyapasiniya wikuwawihkuwak naka nacihpultiniya. Apc kisihpultihtit natokehkiman tokkiw nihi aciyak. Nit yaq-otehc Maliyan 'tahcuwi-macahan, 'sami cuwi-wicuhkekemu wikuwak.

Most of the other children have already gathered around the school when she arrives. Very soon, Mrs. Wellington rings the bell and the children line up to go in. they spend all day in school, until three o'clock, with a break at noontime to go home for lunch. After school Mary Ann goes right home again to help out.

Yut yaq kessahat wikuwak, eci yaq wolimahtek suwitokolasol. Anuwit yaq-ona kis toli-wolaqahqe. Maliyan 'tiyali-qiluwahan mihtaqsol. 'Tiyukul yaq wikuwossol, "Ktotolaskuhyoq pahkak, kihkan eyik. Ktahcuwi yaq monewolawak sqociyik 'sami kis mace-tkeyu."

As she walks into her house she is met by the strong, pleasant smell of sweet grass. There is not only the big coil her mother made yesterday: there is a large bunch of sweet grass, which has been soaked and wrapped in a cloth to keep it damp for braiding. Mary Ann asks where her father is.

Etuciyat yaq Maliyan elomiyat pahkak naci-wicuhkeman mihtaqsol, 'sami 'kosicihtun temonu-te kehtaqsuwok yalapasuwok. Nit-tehc yaq wasisok milcoksewhotiniya naka naci-yalahtuwenomawotultiniya ewehkahahtit sqociyi.

"He's waiting for you out back in the garden," her mother tells her. "You'll have to bring the pumpkins in tonight because it's getting cold."

’Tahcuwi yaq woliyawa naka ’tolihtuwaniya ’siskul, wihton, naka ’tun. Nit ’kihka-kisehtuhtihtit, on yakahc possaqhenomakon ’punomoniya.

Then Mary Ann realizes it’s going to be Halloween tomorrow. She runs quickly out to the garden. The ghosts will be out soon and the children will dress up in old clothes and go out walking with their lighted pumpkins.

Etutapskosilit yaq Maliyan kisikonacil. Wahka-te yaq ’poqanal. Mam-ote yaq kenuk ’peciphal lamikuwam. ’Tiyukul yaq mihtaqsol, “Kamot knaci-yaliphan wot apsapskosossit, not tahk kat-op kisi-yaliphaw ’sami-tkiqol.”

First you have to clean out he pumpkin. Then you cut out the eyes, the nose and the mouth. When you’re finished with that, you put a candle inside and light it.

Saku yaq Maliyan wihqonan apsokilsossilicil nakahc ’punan kinapskosilit qocomok weci yaq psi-te wen nomiyat. Nit ehta-te yaq mihtaqsol macesawan.

Mary Ann’s pumpkin is so huge she can hardly carry it. But finally she gets it into the house.

“You’d better carry this little one around,” her father says, “That one is too heavy.”

On yaq maciyakonutomuwan Maliyanol eleyikpon nekom yaq ewasisuwit. Ma yaq ’tiywawiwa sqociyi. ’Tahcuwi yaq oliyawa pilasqeya, ewekhotihtit yaq utomiley paksis. Pecihc yaq ’tolihtuwaniya ’calokossiyil, naka wihton yaq qeneyik, nakahc ahpapossis weci yaq wen kisi-yaliphat. Maliyan yaq eci-assokitahasit eci yaq mecimi-’tomakeyultihtits pomawsuwinuwok. Itom yaq, “Eci-wolelomoqhotihtit wasisok tokec.”

So Mary Ann decides to put the big one on the front step, where everyone can see it. Her father helps her carve the pumpkins.

“When I was growing up, we didn’t have pumpkins,” says her father. “We had to make them out of oatmeal boxes, with a little string to carry them around by. We even put ears on them—and a long, pointed nose.”

Nit yaq-ote-na wolaqihpultiniya nomehsol, pocetesol, naka mimey.

Mary Ann is surprised that people used to be so poor. She says, “Children today are lucky.”

Ipa, nekka-kossicuweniket Maliyan, nit ehta-te apc wikuwossol maciyacomin. Toke kahk yaq weskuwimacil wahantuwol. Etuci yaq milluhkewinuwit wahant kehsikotok. Eci yaq Maliyan cipomolsit etoli-tpostok.

They have a big supper of fish and potatoes and pork grease. And when Mary Ann is finished with the dishes, her mother starts to tell stories again.

'Tiyal yaq wikuwossol, "Toqc natqahsultine, kehkitin sepawonu." Ipa, kisaqehtit, waht yaq-ote Maliyan peci-wissekhusu, eci yaq mec cipitahasit apeq wihpemal wikuwossol.

Ipa, on spasuwiw natokehkimut, psi yaq-ote wasisok 'totoli-skuhutomoniya eli-koti-yalahsuwenomawolotimok. Wahka-te yaq kiskuwasultuwok tokkiw metokehkitimok. Psi yaq-ote mace-qaskultuwok wikuwawihkuwak, naci-qiluwahtuniya weci wen kisi-milcoksewet. Sqotewamq ewekhotihtit weci wen kisi-moccokikuhusit.

Ipa, kisi-wolaqihpit Maliyan, nit yaq-ote naci-moccokikuhsin naka 'tatsewan. Nekka-kisehlosit, papehk-ote yaq kosqehsuhsis. Nit yaq-ote na 'posqolenan sqocihil, olomi-nuteyya. Nekka-pskuwat witapihi, on yaq 'tiyalamkuhsania. Anqoc yaq-ote tama tolsimuwak sukolisol.

Ipa, nekka-yalkomuhtit wikuwamol on maciyapasiniya wikuwawal. Maliyan yaq cuwi-mace-'qotuhkehe elomawtossok. Eci yaq cipitahasit. Tehpu yaq tepitahamat wahantuwol, on ehta yaq mace-qasqin tan-ote yaq kisi-tuciyat. Eluwe yaq metsonu tokkiw peci-qasqit wikuwak. Kessetqihit, wot-tahk yaq muhsumsol weckuhqepilit. Nit yaq-ote etoli-wonitahasit etutpayitpon.

This time she tells all about the devil and the evil things he had done through the years. Mary Ann gets more and more frightened as she listens to each story. She says, "Let's go to bed. I have to go to school tomorrow."

Even when she's safe in bed with her mother, Mary Ann covers herself up with the blankets because she can't shake off those scary thoughts.

The next morning at school all the children are talking about the evening to come and their procession of candle-lit pumpkins. They can hardly wait until school is out. They'll all run home to look for old clothes to dress up in and stove ashes to blacken their faces.

When Mary Ann is finished with herself she looks just exactly like a little old lady. Lighting the candle in her pumpkin, she hurries out into the dark night to meet her friends. From house to house they go-sometimes they get candy and sometimes they don't. After they visit all the houses, Mary Ann and her friends start for home. Mary Ann has to walk home alone, and she gets so scared thinking about the Devil she starts to run. Faster and faster she runs along the dark road until by the time she gets home she is all out of breath.

She bursts through the door with a great feeling of relief and flops down in a chair by the stove. It isn't until then that she sees her Grandfather sitting at the table. Mary Ann forgets all about being scared.

3

'Toqecimulan muhsumsol keq weci-tuci-metsi-yaliyat. 'Tiyukul yaq, "Npetut, motehsan, 'sami wahka-te kis ntiyali. Ma-te nkisi-piwsokuhkew, ma-na nkisi-ewotapilomu." 'Tiyal, "Yut-olu psi-te keq ktihiniya. Tehpuhc ntolluhk nkossiyewolan tuwanok naka piyaqtihikonisol."

Mary Ann asks her grandfather why he is out so late. He smiles at her. "I've come to live with you, littlest one, because I'm having a hard time now taking care of myself. I can't get firewood or carry water," he says, "but here you have everything. All I'll have to do is bring in the heater wood and the kindling."

Eci-palitahasit Maliyan. Wisokitahamal komac muhsumsol 'sami mecimi-te 'tiyaliphukul kcihkuk naka 'tatkuhkewkun.

Keka yaq muhsumsol 'qotatq tuceyu. Psi yaq-ote kis wapatpe naka ksi-atkiqe.
Ma-te pihcetu kisi-olkawotiwiyik 'sami yaq Muhmumi wahka kisi-yaliye. Qin yaq-ote ckuhqepu qihiw papskotek, minoq-otehc yaq ahtolapotok sqot.

Mary Ann is very happy, because she loves her Grandfather very much. He is almost a hundred years old now, his hair is all white and his face is completely lined with wrinkles. He would always take Mary Ann for walks in the woods and tell her stories. But they can't go far now because Grandfather can hardly walk. Instead, he often spends time sitting near the stove, staring into the flames.

Ecihc yaq ktomakitahamat Maliyan tan eci nit olluhkelit. Ceste yaq 'tolinuwal kiwaciyalit, 'sami pihce yaq uhkomossol mehcinalin. Nit-tehc yaq Maliyan natewestuwaman weci skat yaq ahtoli-tpitahasilihq.

Mary Ann feels sorry for him when she sees him this way. He must be very lonely: her grandmother died a long time ago. Mary Ann goes over to him and talks to him so that he won't have any lonely thoughts.

Kesq yaq nit etolewestuhtit, komotu yaq Anuwit mete-mehqet, nit-te yaq 'sakhiyan Sapatis. 'Tiyal yaq Maliyanol, "Naciphan kikuwoss."

She is sitting with her grandfather when she hears Anna moaning in her bed in the corner. Suddenly, Sabattus comes to Mary Ann and whispers urgently- "Go get you mother."

On yaq Maliyan macahan waht qsokayawtihiw, wikuwossol etolatokonikelit. 'Kisi-yahan eli Anuwit kis mace-ksinuhkat.

Mary Ann hurries across the road to the house where her mother is braiding sweet grass with the other women.

"Anna is starting to have her baby," she says.

'Tiyukul yaq, "Woli-te ehta naciphan kosqehsuhs, nuci-peciphat wasis. Nit-tehc nil nkospestahqan."

Eluwe yaq siktehsonu Maliyan tokkiw peci-qasqit kosqehsuhsok, cel yaq wahka kisewestaq. Nit yaq-ote kosqehsuhs ulacin naka macehkawotiniya. Eci yaq wot kosqehsuhs menakacinaqsit. Maliyan yaq 'tahtoli-wisakiman.

'Tiyal yaq kosqehsuhs, "Ma-te nituwiw kwisahkan, wasis. Mec-otehc petkawotihiq kikuwak. Ktahcuwi-skuhyan pileyahsis. Tan-otehc nekom eci-kisacit, on yakahc nomihqosin."

Mam-ote petkawotihtit, nit yaq-ote wot Maliyan 'kiptahan naka eci-koti-wewisit. 'Tiyukul yaq wikuwossol, "Knostuhmulonc tan etuci-nomihqosit wasis." Ahtolaskuwasit Maliyan naci-kinuwehtuwan, mam-ote yaka spasuwiw wewisu eli yaq mossisol 'qossisilit.

'Toliwiyawal yaq Susehp. Psi yaq-ote mokosewatpe naka kehsok 'piyehsumol, cel yaq kis 'totolihtamuwal Anuwit.

Cuwi yaq Anuwit lossin esqonatek kehsukoniw. Wikuwossol-oc 'tatekewhutolal pileyahsisol naka milan Anuwitol weci-kisihtamuwat.

Yut yaq-ote eltek Anuwit 'kuhutiwa, nit ewepiw lapekessut ehtek. Anuwit yaq wikuwossol kisihtuwat Susehpol ulekiyi naka ahtulhawehsis. Psi yaq-ote palitahasultuwok apc pileyahsis eyit lamikuwam.

"You run and get the old woman," her mother tells her. "I'll heat the water."

Mary Ann is so tired out by the time she gets to the old woman's house she can hardly talk. The old woman, who helps deliver all the babies, gets ready right away and they start back. But she walks so slowly Mary Ann keeps telling her to hurry.

"There's no need to hurry, child," says the old woman patiently, "Even when we get there we'll still have to wait a long time. He won't be born until he's ready."

Finally, they arrive at the house, right away, Mary Ann is sent off to bed.

She wants very badly to stay up to find out about the new baby. Her mother comes to her. "I'll let you know when the baby is born."

Mary Ann waited and waited, until she fell asleep. She never did find out until morning that her sister had had a little boy.

They named him Joseph. He had thick black hair. By the time Mary Ann woke up, Anna was already nursing him. She had to stay in bed for nine days, so her mother took care of the baby and brought him to Anna to be nursed. She made her new grandson his diapers and his little shirts.

Just above Anna's bed hung a cradle-swing across the corner of the room. Joseph slept there and Anna could reach up for him when he woke during the night.

Maliyan yaq natakonutomuwan muhsumsol eli yaq iywahtit pileyahsisol. Wot tahk yaq Muhmumi mec elossit 'topunok. 'Tiyal yaq Maliyanol, "Yahan kikuwoss laqosomuwic skicinuwi-npisun. Possa nutomakomols."

'Kisaqosomuwaniya yaq naka 'kissihpilaniya; kis tahk yaq 'samikotone, ma-te keq 'toli-wolehlokuwon. Nit yaq-ote etolinet ihlossit.

Maliyan wikuwossol 'tapi-pcitaman skitapihi naci yaq wolehlaniya wakat. On petapasihtit, nit-te yaq 'topaskulaniya, 'kospahlaniya, 'posqihtuwahaniya, naka ulehtuwaniya ketuwossinulit. On yaq wot pesq skitap macahan ikolosomanihkuk naka naci-nsotuhmuwan tan cuwi-olkihqon puskonikon.

Nit-tehc ona 'tiyali-maqenikhotiniya weci-kisihpultimok elomi-tpuhkiwik. Nit yaq-ote-na mace-petapasiniya witapihi naka elakumatponhi naci-wici-spasultiniya: 'qoci-tpuhk-otehc tolimiyawolotuwok, tolintuhtuwok tokki-te spasuwiw. On apc maciyapasiniya wikuwawihkuwak tokkiw apc pemolaqik.

Apc naci-wici-spasultiniya. On-oc spasuwiw Muhmumi puskonan. Etuttemultihtit Maliyan naka 'siwihi. Maliyan yaq-ote tolotemu kisi-pasqek. 'Tiyukul yaq wikuwossol, "Kiyasqi nit kesotemiyin. Cuwi psi-te wen mehcine, naka wot Muhmumi kis etuceyit. Sipkiw-ote kwiciyemkun, on yaka-na nekom 'tahcuwi-mehcinan."

Everyone was very happy to have a baby in the house again.

When Mary Ann ran to tell her grandfather about the new baby, she found him still in bed. He said to her, "Tell you mother to cook me some Indian medicine. I feel very poorly."

They cooked the medicine for him and gave him some. But Grandfather was too old. It didn't do him any good. He died in his bed.

Mary Ann's mother sent for the men who would prepare Grandfather's body for burial. They washed him and shaved him. After that, they fixed a place in the house for him to lie. One of the men measured him and went over to Princeton to have a casket made.

As soon as they find out about the death, all the neighbors gather food for the wake. Friends and relatives arrive. They pray and sing all night until early in the morning. Then everyone goes home to rest before the second night of the wake.

The following morning, Grandfather is buried. Mary Ann and her family are crying very hard. Even in the afternoon, Mary Ann is still crying. "You have cried enough," her mother tells her.

"Everyone must die, and Grandfather was very old. He was with us for a long time before he had to leave."

Etoli-wolaqihpultihtit, Maliyan mihtaqsol 'totoli-skuhutomon eli yaq temonu-te pkonut sakom. Maliyan yaq ma-te witewestu tuwihputik, kenoq ma yaq-ona toke sasotemiw. 'Kosicihtun yaq toke weci-mehcinet Muhmumi.

At supper, Mary Ann's father is talking about the election soon to be held. She doesn't join in the conversation, but she isn't crying now. She understands why Grandfather died.

4

Ipa, mam-ote cuwi-pkona sakom. On yaq Maliyan mihtaqsol 'totolacin keti-naci-pkonat nekom welitahamacil. Wot-olu yaq Maliyan eci-kci-wewisuwit. 'Tiyal yaq mihtaqsol, "Mec-op-al-na nil kisi-macephi?"

It is time to pick a new chief; Mary Ann's father has decided whom to vote for. By now, Mary Ann is very curious and excited about the election. "Take me with you," she begs her father.

'Tiyukul yaq, "Woli-te ckuwi, motehsan."

"Come along, then, little one," he says.

On yaq macehkawotiniya. Waht petkawotihtit, yuktok nisuwok skitapiyik weckuhqepihtit, Tepit naka Oluwi. On yaq mihtaqsol monehtun 'tahsosuwon naka 'tolahkan yet oloqiw epit Tepit. Ipa, on 'taskuwasiniya.

When they arrive at the voting place at Peter Dana Point, the two candidates, David and Louis, are sitting on chairs at opposite ends of the room. There are hats all around their feet. Mary Ann's father takes his hat off and throws it on the floor near David. Then they stand back and wait.

On Maliyan 'toqecikesin keq mehsi mihtaqsol lahket 'tahsosuwon Tepit oloqiw epit.

"Why did you throw your hat on the floor?" Mary Ann asks her father.

'Tiyukul yaq, "Not-te peyemi-miyawitahamuk 'sakomawin. Ktahcuwihc skuwasipon okitasu ahsosuwonol. Tan wot peyemihtaq, not-oc temhuwet."

"David is the one I think will make the best chief," says her father. "Now we have to wait until the hats are counted. The one with the most hats will be chief."

Ipa, mam-ote kisokitasuwol ahsosuwonol. Oluwi yaq-ote peyemihtaq. Psi yaq-ote skitapiyik 'tolapasiniya naci-sokiptinenaniya naka 'tehsahqehlaniya 'tolomakonuwak temhuwelit. Wolitahasultuwok. Nit-te-na yaq mote-peskote kci-peskuwat.

At last the hats are counted. Louis had more than David. All of the men congratulate him. They shake his hand and carry him aloft on their shoulders, happy for his victory.

Ipa, nit-ehta-te mawessultiniya pomawsuwinuwok, keti-nastuhut sakom. Peskuwok skitapiyik

Someone sets off the cannon down by the shore to announce the election of a new chief. Preparations begin for the inauguration. Men go hunting. There will be a big feast with stew for everyone. Each family brings a pot and

naci-kotunkahtiniya, weci-kisi-wiqhopaltimok. Psi-tehc yaq pomawsuwin kisapuwe. Nit-tehc na pemolaqik sakomawkan naka wiwonosihmawotin sukolisol, cikonihik, naka pokansisol.

Waht-oc yaq kikociw sehket Asseloma. Nekom yaq nuci-kotuhmahsit naka nucintaq. Ipa, tan etuci 'kihka-kisacultihtit, nit-tehc yaq mace-nskawan naka nspiw 'tolomi-menakacuhsan sakomal epilit.

Tan etuci pecuhset waht epilit, on-oc 'tiyan, "Nulasihkuwa pili-sakom."

Nit-tehc yaq toqc psi-te wen mace-skicinuwokan. Tan etuci Asseloma mace-kotuhmahsit, psi-tehc wen wonaku naka 'pomokan. Eci-'tawi-kotuhmahsit. Neqt 'sonte-tehc qonkan, naka ma-tehc oluwawotultiwiyik. Eci-tehc wolokamok.

Wasisok tahk yaq miyahsi-macehtahak: nit tehpu yaq Maliyan weciluwahat. Kenoq yaq mahkiyew kisokehkimsu elkat. Eci yaq woli-tpinuwat wikuwossol etolokalit, on yaq 'toqetokehkoluhtuwan. 'Tiyukul yaq wikuwossol, "Kuli-kiseht, wasis. Nit-te ktotolokehkimsin, temonu-tehc-ona kil ecihc 'tawkayin."

Eci-palitahasit Maliyan nit yuhut, on yaq 'taqami-palessin.

takes stew home to eat; candy, apples and nuts will be given out.

There is a great dance in honor of the new chief. Mary Ann sees an old man named Samuel standing in the corner. She knows that he's the one who beats the drum and sings. When all is ready, the Welcome Dance begins. In time to the beat of his drum and his chant, Samuel walks very slowly to where the new chief sits on the floor.

"I welcome the new chief," he says, and shakes his hand.

Then all the people shout and they begin to dance. All night, whenever Samuel takes up the drum and begins to sing, everyone dances. He really knows how to beat the drum.

The dance goes on for a whole week without anyone getting into trouble. While the adults all have a grand time at the celebration, the children are sent home early. That's the only thing Mary Ann doesn't like, but she does get to dance for a little while. She practices her dancing by watching her mother very closely and trying to imitate her every movement.

"You do very well," her mother tells her. "You keep practicing and soon you'll be a very good dancer."

Mary Ann was so proud to hear her mother's praise that she tired even harder.

Mahkiyew-ote kiska, nit-te-na 'tahcuwi-macahan. Tehpu yaq toke kci-pomawsuwinuwok ketuwokawolotihtit.

She danced for just a little longer, then she had to go home. Only the adults would be dancing during the night.

Eci-ehta ktonukahk kisi-sakomawkamok; komac-oc sipkiw yaka Maliyan unitahasin.

The inauguration of the chief was a very important ceremony. It would be a long time before Mary Ann forgot it.

5

Ipa, mam-ote yaq kis keka puniw. Maliyan yaq nihtaqsol kis api-punawe. Kestahat yaq kiwhosu, on-oc apc yaq naci-kotunkan. Apc-oc yaq kehsok otuhkey.

Susehp yaq-ona etutahqekonasit weci skat siktewocihq. Kis yaq elkilok. Nit yaq elapewit tahalu wikuwossol; tehpu 'toli-oluwahkamal mihtaqsol elocihtek 'piyehsumol.

Itom Maliyan, "Pal toqc Senotihkolas peciyat. Nkoti-nomiya Susehp tan 'tolluhkan Nipayimiyamk."

Wikuwossol 'tiyukul, "Ehqi-te wisahk. Ktahcuwi-tehc skuwas tokkiw Nipayimiyamk." Maliyan yaq tuhkiyat spasuwiw, kis yaq etuci-psak. 'Tahcuwi yaq psihkuwa 'tolapasom natokehkimut naka pahsekilicil 'toptanol. Eci-wolinok Maliyan etoli-psak. Eci yaq menakacuhset elomiyat etolokehkitimok.

Pasqekil, on yaq 'toliyaniya wasisok wastewi-amsqocehkanol. Elkilulit yaq kisiyahticil. Nit-te yaq weci-mace-wastewihkek. Mam-ote metokehkitin yaq, nanukoniw: keti-Nipayimiyamok.

On yaq Maliyan naka mihtaqsol naciphaniya stahqonul weci-kisi-punahtit lamikuwam. Maliyan yaq kis 'kisekisomonol pilasqeyal ekhutaq stahqonuk. Eci yaq milahkukahk naka eci-milocihtek. Apaciphahtit stahqonul,

Cold weather came and Mary Ann's father set out his traps. He caught many muskrat. Later, during hunting season there would be a good supply of venison in the house.

Joseph was well wrapped up against the cold. He was quite big now and looking a lot like his mother, except that he had his father's hair.

Mary Ann said, "I wish Santa Claus would come. I want to see what Joseph does on Christmas!"

"Don't be in such a hurry," says her mother. "You will just have to wait until Christmas comes."

When Mary Ann wakes up in the morning, it is snowing very hard. She has to wear her rubbers and her heavy coat to school. Because the snow is so beautiful to look at, Mary Ann walks very slowly on her way.

At lunch-time on these snowy days all the children make a snowman. Sometimes they make a very big one.

Not too long after the first snow came a week of vacation-for Christmas.

Mary Ann and her father went to get a tree for the house. She had been spending quite a bit of time cutting paper ornaments. They were of all different shapes and pretty colors.

mihtaqsol 'kisihtun ihtolikapuwilit. On kisi-puwaqtahahtit, 'kossephaniya. Susehp eci-milapomat Maliyanol etoli-nassewhutolat stahqonul. 'Tahtolelomin nekom. Nokosanaqot Maliyan 'kiseyin. Eci-wolinaqsit stahqon nekka-kisehlut.

Mary Ann's father had made a place for the fir tree to stand. When they brought it back, they brushed off the snow and carried it into the house. Joseph kept staring at Mary Ann with big round eyes as she trimmed the tree. In no time, she had it all decorated. Joseph laughed with delight, for the tree was so beautiful to see.

Nit yaq-ote-na naciptun saks naka 'tekhutun qihiw khakonok. Nit yaq-ote-na natqahsinon, 'sami 'kosicihtun tokec 'sami-metsi-spasit, ma-tehc Senotihkolas peciyew. Sipkiw yaq 'tolossinon kuhutik, 'tahtoli-tpitahatomon yaq naci-kikimapoman Senotihkolasol peciyalit elomi-tpuhkik. Nit yaq-ote etoloqsit.

Then Mary Ann went to get a sock to hand up by the door. She went right to bed because she knew that if she stayed up too late, Santa Claus wouldn't come. For a long time she lay in her bed, thinking she might go have a peek at Santa when he arrived at midnight. But before she knew it, Mary Ann fell asleep.

Apc yaq tuhkiyat, kis yaq cehqot. Nit yaq-ote wetamihkiyat, macahan stahqonul epilit. Wot-tahk yaq amsqocehkan weckuhqepit neqiw, saks yaq-ona psonte-te pokansisol, sukolisol, cikonihik: eci-ehta yaq milinaqahk. Susehp yaq-ona piley 'tolayyektakon, eci yaq milapotok.

By the time she woke up, it was already light. She hopped out of bed and ran over to the tree. There was a little doll sitting underneath it, and her stocking was filled to the top with nuts, candy, and apples- so many things! Joseph had a new toy too, and he looked at it very strangely.

Nit yaq-ote naci-witimiyawolotiniya. Naci-wolasuweltomultiniya etuci-wolelomoqekhat Sesuhs.

Soon it was time to go to church to thank Jesus for all their good fortune.

'Kekiw yaq-ote Maliyan 'totolayyekhal 'tamsqocehkanol, eci yaq palitahasit. Ehemuwol yaq-ona kisi-pasqihipultihtit. Etuci yaq-ote wolemoqhotihtit Nipayimiyamok, Sesuhs etuci-mihqositpon.

Mary Ann is very pleased with her doll. She plays with it all day. And there is chicken for Christmas dinner. They are a very fortunate family at Christmas time, the birthday of the Christ child.

6

Maliyan yaq mihtaqsol 'totolacilin 'sami yaq oliye Sipayik, on yaq-ona Maliyan 'koti-macephoqan. Mesq yaq-ote nekom nit uciyawon.

'Tiyukul yaq mihtaqsol, "Ktahcuwihc olkawotipon utenek, nit-oc weci-macephukiyiq kasok tokkiw Kelisk. Apc kotok kas ktepessinen tokkiw etoli-esuwi-tepessultimok. Nit apc weci-macephukiyiq tokkiw Sipayik.

Waht peciyahtit eci Maliyan milapit. Ma-te yaq nit 'kehsiwoniya oposiyik tahalu nekomaw wikihtit, naka yaq elkihqahk lontoq. 'Tiyukul yaq mihtaqsol, "Supeq nit." Eci Maliyan assokitahasit eli skat kolotonunuhk.

On yaq 'tolkawotiniya Kci-Malihk. Eci-wolitahasit 'tantimol. Nit yaq-ote 'tapuwisawan naka macephan wahsiw messunomuwan 'topunuwal. Kisihpihtit, on yaq mihtaqsol naci-qiluwahan witapiyil weci-apamehtit naka nspiw 'cuspeskaniya, tokec woluwipok spasuwiw.

Apc yaka spasuwiw Maliyan tuhkiye. Cel yaq kis 'tantimol kisahqe, pocetesol naka nomehs. Etucihpit Maliyan, nit-te-na yaq 'koti-naci-yaliyan.

'Tiyukul 'tantimol, "Ktahcuwi-nahsonomon elamkomonil, 'sami tkeyu yut oloqiw." 'Kekiw yaq-ote Maliyan yaliye. Mam-ote mihtaqsol 'peci-naciphukul.

Mary Ann's father is getting ready to go to Pleasant Point and Mary Ann wants to go with him. She's never gone there before.

"It will take us all day." Her father tells her. "We'll have to walk into town. There we'll get on the train and ride as far as Calais. Then we get on another train to Ayers Junction, where we change again for Pleasant Point."

Mary Ann stares all around when they arrive at Pleasant Point. There aren't nearly as many trees as they have at home- and look how big the lake is!

"That's salt water," her father tells her. Mary Ann is surprised that it's not frozen over.

From the railroad station they walk to Old Mary's. Mary Ann's aunt is very glad to see them. She warms up some food and takes them in to show them their beds.

After they have supper, Mary Ann's father goes off to look for his friend. They might go fishing if it's nice in the morning, and at the same time go after porpoise.

Mary Ann wakes up to the smell of potatoes and fish cooking on the stove. She eats her breakfast quickly because she wants very much to go out and walk around.

Her aunt tells her, "You'll have to put on your long-johns—it's very cold down here."

'Tiyal yaq, "Kamot knaci-wolaqihpin naka ktatolahsimin. Sepawonu kwesuwessipon."

Mam-ote kisi-wolaqihpultihtit, on mihtaqsol 'takonutomakun kehsi-nehpahahtit cuspes, 'Koti yaq nihiht salawehlawa. 'Qoci-pun-otehc yaq nihiht 'tolapemawa.

On yaq 'tantimol 'posqolenomon possaqhenomakon naka motutuwan. Eci yaq wolopotek. On natqepin 'tolapekessutik; Maliyan yaq ckuhqepu emehkew. Nit-te yaq maciyacomin eli yaq yali-nomiyut pihtenskosit wen nipayiw. Eci yaq Maliyan cipalokiqewit, 'tahtolapin possiyanteskik.

Mam-ote 'tantimol naci-kpekopolike. Eltaqahk yaq metelamsok qocomok. Apc yaq Maliyan 'taqami-cipitahasin. Etutapekiyat yaq 'tantimol, cel yuhtol utomakonol. Mam-ote yaq 'tiyukul, "Nehe, wasis, kamot toqc knatqahsinunen."

'Kisi-'kahsuwehtuniya possaqhenomakon, macehkawotiniya wahsiw. Eci yaq wolopotek 'topunuwa.

Spasuwiw on yaq wesuwessiniya nolomok. Eci-wikuwatacqiphut kasok. Mam-ote peciphak utenek, macehkawotiniya wikuwak. Wolitahasultuwok Maliyan 'siwihi eli-apaciyahtit. Maliyan yaq-ote 'possonapin wikuwak, cestehp yaq api-sipki-macahat.

Mary Ann spends her day outside. Finally her father comes after her. "You'd better go have supper and rest. We have to go back tomorrow."

After they eat, he tells her about going hunting and about all the porpoise they killed. They are going to salt them, he says, so that they'll have them all winter.

Auntie lights the lamp and puts more wood in the stove. It is warm and comfortable in this house. Mary Ann sits on the floor near her aunt's rocking chair. Old Mary tells the story of the Tall Man who is seen sometimes at night. Mary Ann's eyes grow wider and she keeps glancing at the window. Finally her aunt puts a blanket over the panes, but the wind is so loud that Mary Ann is still afraid. Old Mary rocks back and forth, her pipe in her mouth.

"Well, child," she says, "we'd better go to bed."

They put out the lamp and walk into the other room. It is cozy in their big warm bed.

In the morning Mary Ann and her father go back up to Princeton. It's fun to ride on the train, but Mary Ann is glad when they arrive in town and start walking home.

Her family are all glad to see them. Mary Ann looks all around the house, as if she has been gone for a very long time.

'Tolapoman wikuwossol naka mihtaqsol naka Anuwitol, Susehpol. On yaq 'titomon, "Eci-wolelomoqhotiyiq kilun. Ktepihtunen micuwakon, kuloposultipon-ona, naka koselomotultinen."

Nit-te psiw.

She looks at her mother and father, at Anna and little Joseph. And she smiles, "We are very lucky. We have enough food, our house is warm, and we all love one another."

That's all.

Kuhkomossonuk Akonutomuwinokot

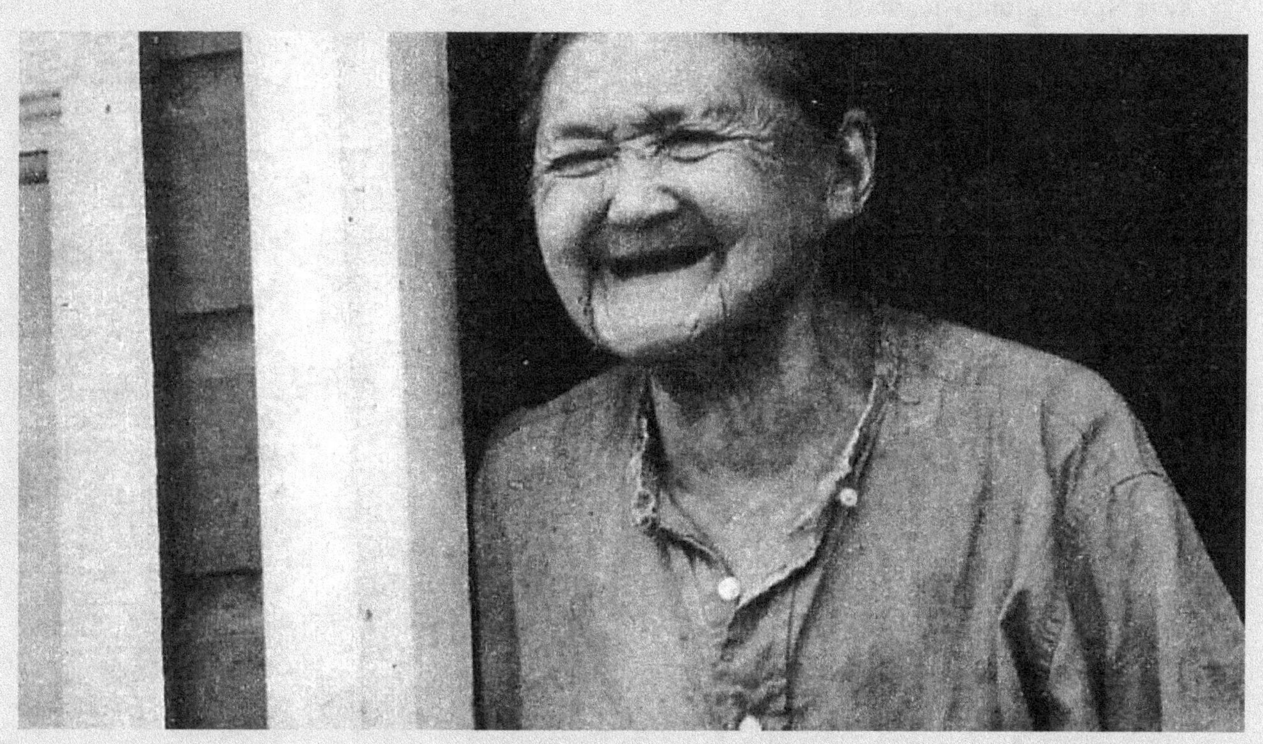

Stories Our Grandmothers Told Us

Kuhkomossonuk Akonutomuwinokot: Stories Our Grandmothers Told Us

Amucalu — The Fly (as told by Elizabeth Newell)

Mahtoqehs naka Malsom — Hare and Wolf (Elizabeth Newell from oral tradition)

Akonutomuwin — Tell Me a Story (Mary Ellen Stevens Socobasin, Elizabeth Lacoote, Wayne Newell, John Nicholas)

- Wonakomehsis — The Little Person
- Eniqs — Ant
- Sikiliyem — Cricket
- Sqotes naka Apiqsehsis — Spark and Mouse

Wahant — Devil Stories (Irene Newell, Elizabeth Newell, and Lorraine Gabriel)

- Kihke Wahant — The Devil Plants a Garden
- Nutapektuhusit — The Fiddler
- Tolamotultuwok — The Card-players
- Moci-ehpit — The Evil Woman
- Witimiye Wahant — The Devil Goes to Church
- Wisawi-maniyeyal Sopiqonol — Golden Tears
- Suwahqihike — The Bell Rings
- Papahtomuwewtimok — Praying
- Etolispasultimok — At the Wake

Kehtaqs — Ghost Stories (Irene Newell)

- Antiw — Auntie (My Late Aunt)
- Ktopinaq Wahant — The Devil Is Watching You
- Kehtaqsuwok — Ghosts
- Motewolon — The Motewolon (person with extraordinary spiritual powers)
- Kepcicuwok — At the Narrows
- Sqotewi-ahahs — The Fiery Horse

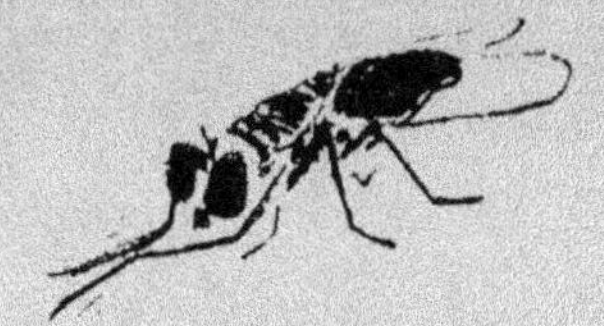

Amucalu

The Fly

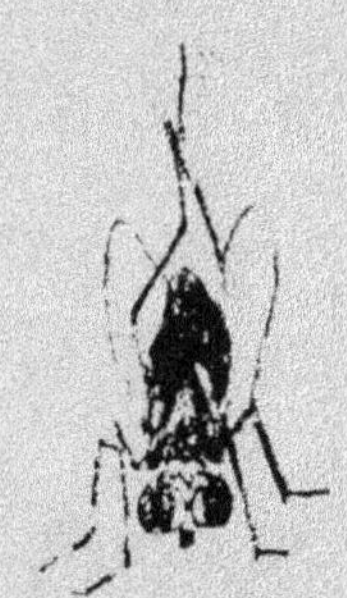

as told by Elizabeth Newell
photographs and illustrations by Robert M. Leavitt

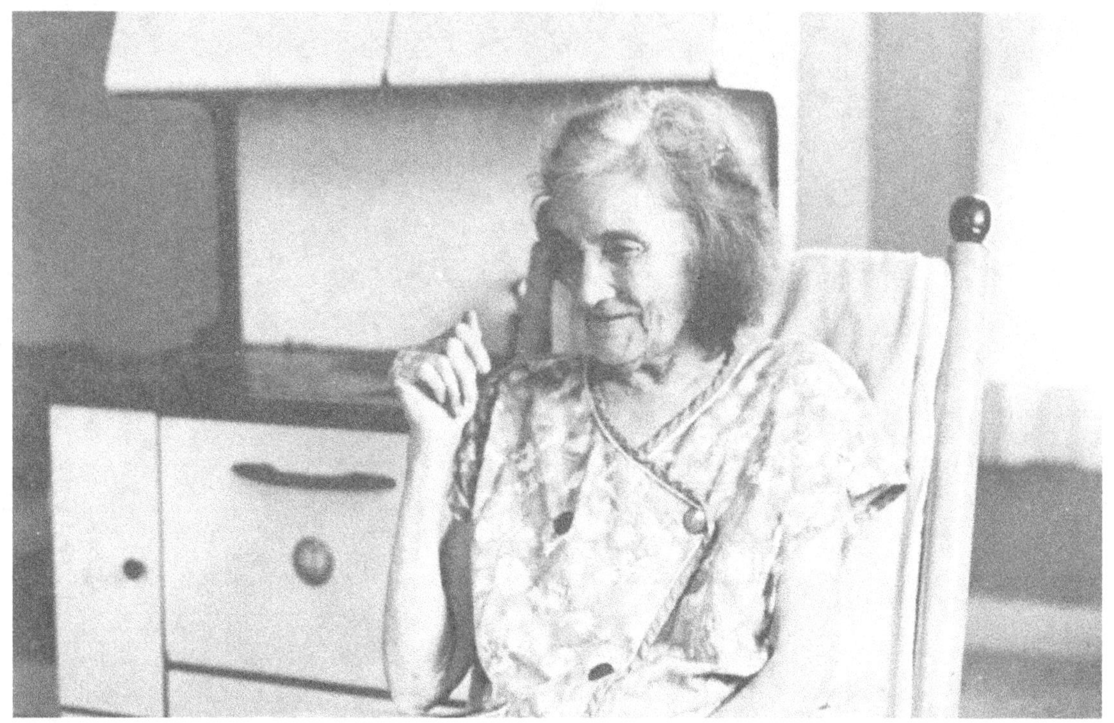

Kis knomiyawa amucalu etoli-kossiqensit?

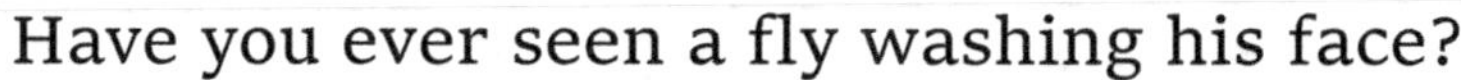

Have you ever seen a fly washing his face?

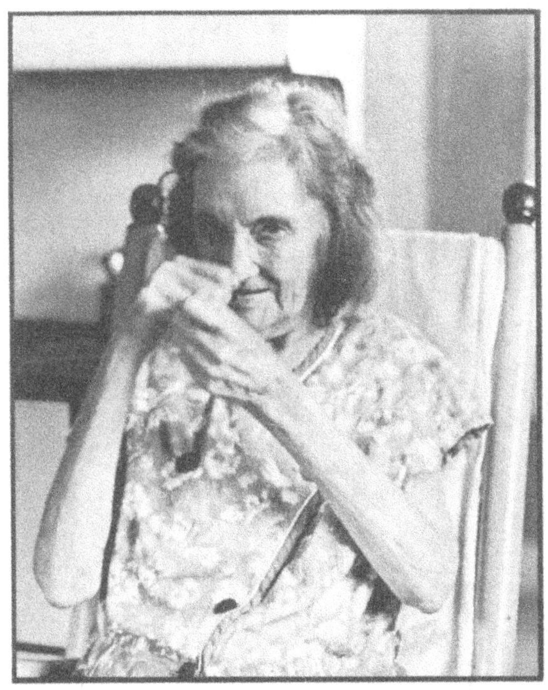

Kessiqensit, nit 'tolehtunol 'pihtinol.

When he washes his face, he does that with his hands.

Apc nit 'tolehtun 'pihtinol.

And then he does that with his hands.

Apc elehtaq 'pihtinol, usami-kossiqensin, on 'tomiqehlosin. Tette olomamuwe woniyakon.

When he does that again with his hands, he washes his face too much, and his head comes off. And his head rolls away over there.

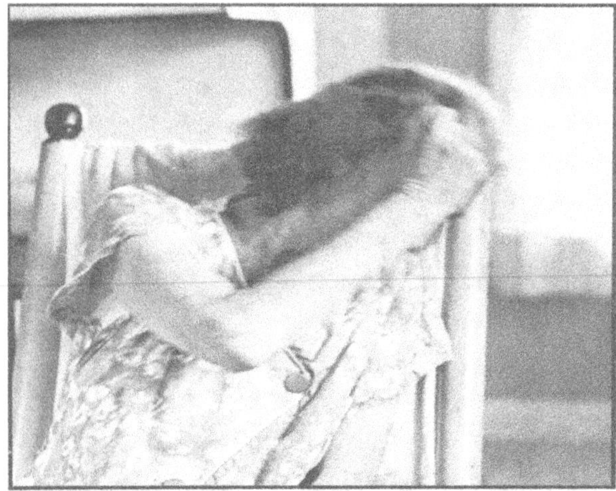

Weckuhqepit ma-te woniyakoniw.

He's sitting there without any head!

Nit-te psiw.

That's all.

Mahtoqehs naka Malsom

Hare and Wolf

as told by Elizabeth Newell from oral tradition
illustrations by Faye Hoban

Wot yaq mahtoqehs naka coqols tama-al kcihkuk etolakonutomahtit. 'Tiyal yaq wot mahtoqehs coqolsol, "Tan-op kil ktolluhkan tokec ckuwi-motahat ya malsom?"

Once this hare and a frog were somewhere in the woods telling stories. The hare said to the frog, "What would you do if you heard a wolf coming this way?"

I... coqols yut yaq-ote 'tiyali-kcitacokessin iyik ososqihkuk, etoli-kalsit. 'Tiyal yaq mahtoqehsuwol, "Kil-op-olu tan ktolluhkan?"

Eee... the frog was burrowing into the mud, hiding. He said to the hare, "What would you do?"

Kesq yaq nit etolakonutomahtit, komotu weckuwi-motehtaqsit malsom. Coqahk-al coqols olomi-kcitassuwa yut iyik ososqihkuk. Yat-olu mahtoqehs 'kisi-pkikatomon piyaqtihikonisol—nohonul. On yaq mace-qasqin, macephuwan.

While they were talking, suddenly a wolf was heard approaching. Of course the frog buried himself in the mud. That hare grabbed the wood-chips—three of them. And he started to run, he took off.

Wot-olu malsom peciyat, coqahk-al 'possahal coqolsol; tehpu qeni-walket, nit-te nokkalan nihtol. On elomaptaq mahtoqehs, on macephoqan.

But when the wolf arrived, of course he smelled the frog; he just dug, and then he ate him up. And the hare ran off, leaving tracks, and the wolf started after him.

Wot-olu mahtoqehs pemiptaq nohonul piyaqtihikonol. Solahkiw yaq-ote ciksotok mahtoqehs yat kis wecuwawoss ckuwi-motehtaqsu malsom. On yaq 'tolahkan piyaqtihikon, nomocini-awtik. 'Tolahkan. I... yut-tahk yaq wikuwam ehtek, on nekom 'kossahan.

This hare was carrying three wood-chips. All of a sudden, when he listened, the wolf could be heard getting very close. And he threw a wood-chip by the side of the road. He threw it. And there, suddenly, stood a house, and he went into it.

I... cel yaq 'tolekopisuwon, wapekon 'tahsosuwon, psi-te wapsewe (wapeyu ipocol mahtoqehs), psi-te wapsewe. On iyey etolahqet, ceste cestehsit wot ya malsom. 'Kossetqihin.

Eee... and he had an apron on, and his hat was white, he was all dressed in white (because a hare is white), all dressed in white. And as he was cooking, it was as if the wolf appeared out of nowhere. He came right in.

’Tiyal yaq mahtoqehsuwol, “Ma-te tama knomiyaw mahtoqehs yut tuciyew?”

He said to the hare, “Haven’t you seen a hare go by anywhere around here?

’Tiyal yaq, “I... ipal elinaqsit ehtahsokiskahkil etutapasicik yut.”

He said to him, “Eee... so many of them go by here every day.”

“Kat kahk niktok. Nit tahk elikit, papehk-ote.”

“Not those. He looks just like that, exactly.”

’Tiyal yaq, “Kotama.” ’Tiyal yaq, “Pol-opin, atolahsim.”

He told him, “No.” He told him, “You should sit down and rest.”

I... ’kis-opin malsom. ’Kisi-milan yut yey ti tuwossomutossisok, naka tuciw ihik kolehkossisok. ’Tiyal, “Pol mits.”

Eee... the wolf sat down. He gave him this tea in a little cup, and besides some little crackers. “First, eat,” he said.

He was eating, the wolf, and then he fell

Wot-olu etolihpit, malsom, nit-te etoloqsit. Mahtoqehs uci-macahan. Wot-olu tuhkiyat, weckuhqepit tama-al ososqihkuk. Eci ehta mocinaqahk etoli-tuhkiyat. Psonopulce yaq-ote iyil mahtoqehs wocisol, naka yet mahtoqehs 'sokiwon nit-te-na tuwossomutossisok ehtek. On yaq 'sukayahkan, etuciluwahat. "Mocahantuwi-mahtoqehs!" Apc macephoqan.

asleep. The hare left that place. When the wolf woke up, he was sitting somewhere in the mud. It was awful-looking where he woke up. He had a handful of hare turds, and that hare urine was right there in the little cup. And he threw it out, he was so mad. "That devilish hare!" And he took off after him again.

Solahkiw-ote apc wot mahtoqehs nutuwal apc weckuwi-wecuwawsit. Apc 'tolahkan piyaqtihikon. I... yut-tahk yaq imiyewikuwam ehtek. Nekom yaq pahtoliyas cel yaq wapatpe, nihkaniw tolimiye.

Suddenly the hare heard him getting closer again. Again he threw a wood-chip. Eee... here stood a church. He was the priest, with white hair, and he was at the front, praying.

Kessetqihit ya malsom, woli-te noqcihkuwal. 'Tiyal, "Ma-te tama knomiyaw mahtoqehs yut tuciyew?"

When the wolf jumped in he went straight up to him. He said, "Haven't you seen a hare going by here anywhere?

'Tiyal yaq wot pahtoliyas, "Menakac... tolimiyan yut."

The priest said to him, "Quiet... there are prayers being said here."

On apc yaq nanakiwoss 'tiyal yaq, "Ma-te mahtoqehs yut tuciyew?"

And after a little while, he said to him, "Didn't a hare go by here?"

'Tiyal yaq, "Menakac... tolimiyan yut."

He told him, "Quiet... they're praying here."

Kesq yaq wot etoli-ciksotok etolimiyamok, on 'kuwin. Apc mahtoqehs uci-macahan. On apc tuhkiyat wot malsom, eci sikipisokek tama-al, wahka yaq uci-muskapekin.

On yaq apc macephoqan, wot-olu

While he was listening to the prayers, he fell asleep. Again the hare took off. And when the wolf woke up again, he was somewhere in a thicket and could hardly crawl out.

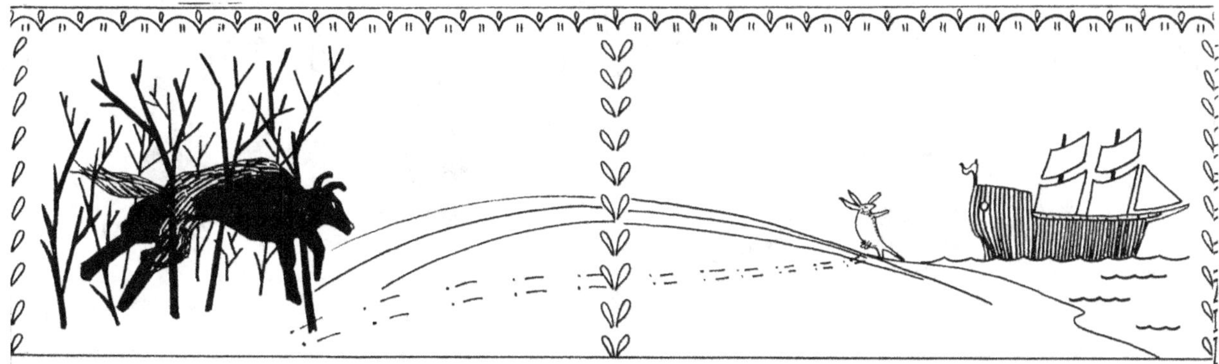

mahtoqehs pcossol pesqon eyit piyaqtihikon. Solahkiw-ote wecuwawsotuwal apc, nit-te-na motapahan sitomok. Tama-al sitomok metapahat, on 'cuwahpahkan yey yut piyaqtihikon. Nit-te-na 'tehsaqotoqqin. Yut-tahk yaq motapekuloq elkihqahk. Nit-te etoli-esuwuhset wot ya keptin.

And again he took off after him, but the hare had only one wood-chip left. Suddenly he heard him getting near again, and then he ran down to the shore. When he came down to the shore somewhere, then he threw the wood-chip into the water. And then he jumped on top of it. Here was a huge warship. There was this captain, walking back and forth.

Wot-olu metape-qasqit ya malsom, 'tahtoli-wathikan. 'Tiyal yaq, "Nathulin!" On 'taphulan.

When the wolf ran down, he kept waving to him. He said, "Take me aboard!" And he came for him in a boat.

Weckuhqepit tepiw yut ihik motapekulokuk. On yey keptinol 'toqecimulan, "Ma-te knomiyaw mahtoqehs yut tuciyew?"

There he was sitting aboard the warship. And he asked the captain, "Haven't you seen a hare go by here?"

'Tiyal yaq, "Elinaqsit alapasicik."

He said to him, "A lot of them wander by here."

"Kat kahk niktok." 'Kisi-yahan papehk-ote elikilit.

"Not those." He told him exactly what he looked like.

'Tiyal, "Kotama. Mesq-ote nomiyaw." Ahtoli-esuwuhset wot, ahtoli-esuwuhset.

He said, "No. I haven't seen him yet." He kept walking back and forth, back and forth.

Solahkiw yaq-ote malsom 'tiyal yaq yuhtol keptinol, "Mehsi nit kil tutalokiqayin?" (ipocol mahtoqehs kinalokiqe).

Suddenly the wolf said to the captain, "Why do you have such big eyes?" (because hares do have big eyes).

'Tiyal yaq, "Yut ehta kehsi-laputihiki etolihponoltimok 'somakonossok psi niktok, nit weci-macekok nsiskul."

He said, "From looking so much through binoculars at all those soldiers fighting, that's why my eyes started to grow."

Eci-assokitahasit wot malsom. Solahkiw yaq-ote 'tiyal yaq yey, "Keq-olu mehsi nit olkihqahk kcalokossiyil?" (ipocol mahtoqehs kinalokosse).

The wolf was so surprised. Suddenly he said to him, "But why are your ears so big?" (because hares do have big ears).

"Kehsi-ciksotom nit yey, etolihponoltimok."— Assokitahasit yaq.

"From listening so much to the fighting."— He was surprised.

"Keq-olu nit mehsi-olcoksitayin?" (ipocol mahtoqehs stehpal qaqeyik yuhtol 'qatol). "Mehsi nit olcoksitayin?"

"Why is it that your feet are dirty?" (because hares' feet are kind of dirty-looking). "Why are your feet so dirty?"

'Tiyal mahtoqehs, "Yuktok nit nusomakonossomok yalosomsqahtihtit 'tomawey. Nit nil eqcuhsi, weci-moccoksitay."

The hare told him, "These soldiers of mine spit tobacco all over the place. When I walk on it, that's why I get dirty feet."

'Tiyal yaq, "Mehsi-olu nit qonahqaluwahsiyin?"

He said to him, "Why is your tail so short?"

'Tiyal yaq, "Neke ehta pisatuwiyan yut lahkapok, on kpotehtehson kpihikon. Nit etoli-tomahqaluwehtuhuki."

He said, "A long time ago when I was hurrying down the hatch, the lid slammed. That's how my tail got cut off."

Coqahk-al wot malsom etoli-assokitahasit, nit-te apc etoloqsit. Weci-macahat mahtoqehs. Wot-olu weckuwi-tuhkiyat yalpektihiket, nit-te etoli-pucoqossit.

Of course the wolf was surprised, and then he fell asleep again. The hare left that place. When the wolf woke up, he was splashing around, and there he drowned.

Akonutomuwin

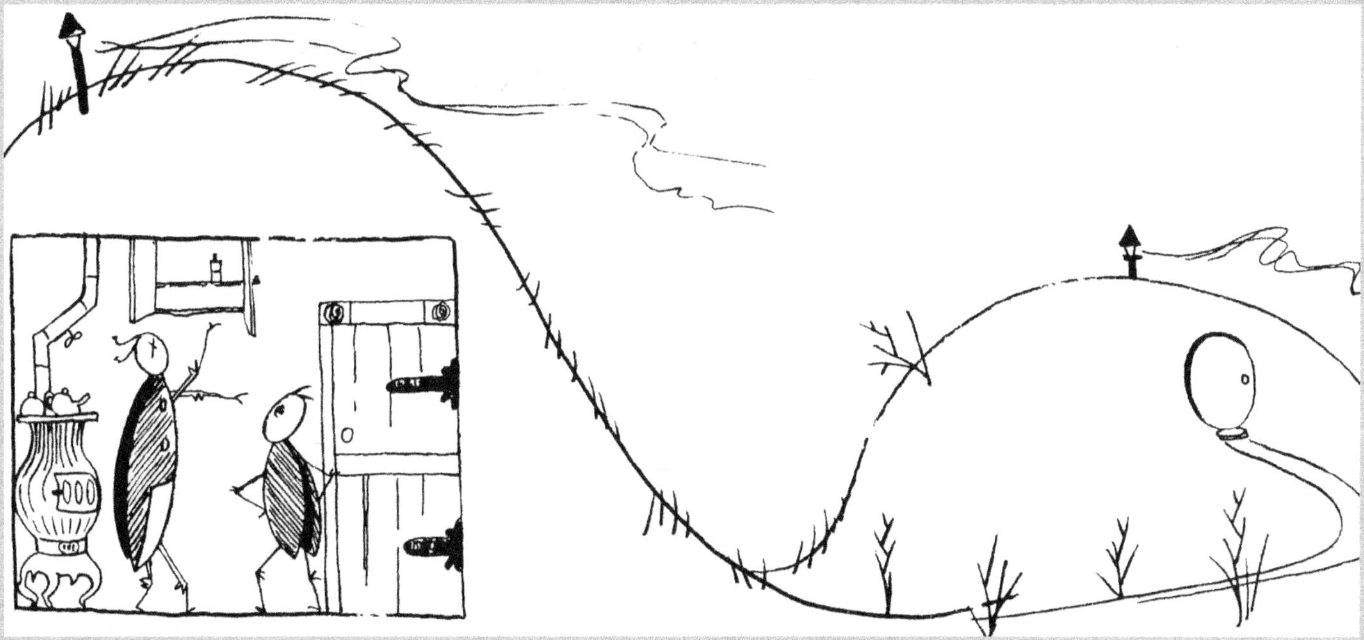

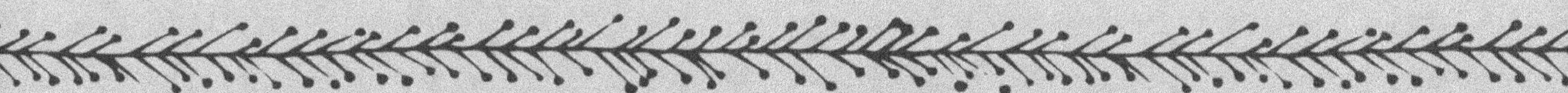

Tell Me a Story

Akonutomuwin — Tell Me a Story

Wonakomehsis — The Little Person (as told by Mary Ellen Stevens Socobasin)
Eniqs — Ant (as told by Elizabeth Lacoote and Wayne A. Newell)
Sikiliyem — Cricket (as told by Elizabeth Lacoote and Wayne A. Newell)
Sqotes naka Apiqsehsis— Spark and Mouse (as told by John Nicholas)

Illustrations by Faye Hoban

Wonakomehsis

The Little Person

as told by **Mary Ellen Stevens Socobasin**

Neqt wot ehpit 'qotuhkanu; puniw nit neke. Etutaqahtek. Komotu sesolahkiw-ote wen mete-puwaksontuhusit. Nit-te-na wen 'tapotehlan 'takom nomociniw wikuwamok.

Once this woman lived alone; it was winter then. The snow was so deep. All of a sudden she heard someone brushing the snow off his boots. And then someone leaned his snowshoes against the side of the house.

Apqotessok khakon, nit-te wen 'sakhiksahan, nukcihkomon te papskot. I!... etoloposusit. Ma yaq-ote wot ehpit kisimacessiw, eci-siktehpayit.

The door opened, and then someone came right in and went straight for the stove. Eee... he was warming himself. The woman couldn't move, she was so frightened.

Mam-ote yaq wot wonakomehsis kisoposusit, 'tolomi-nutahan. Mote-nahsonan 'takom, nit-te-na 'tolomi-motahan. On yaka wot ehpit 'kisamihkin. On 'kisapqotehtun khakon. Ma-te tama wonakomehsis olomaptu. Nit-te etoli-ksihkassit.

Finally, when this little person had warmed himself, he went out. She heard him putting on his snowshoes, and then he could be heard going away. And at that point the woman got up. And she opened the door. Nowhere had the little person left any tracks. He had disappeared.

Eniqs — Ant

as told by **Elizabeth Lacoote** and **Wayne A. Newell**

Not ehta yaq eniqs pemiyat, sopayiw pomiye. Wot yaq elomiyat. Nomiya okamok etoli-epeskomhotilicihi. Nita, tan toke 'toli-kisi-qsokassin?
Nekom-ona koti-wici-epeskome.
(On-al toke miyawikin!)

That ant, they say, was going along, going along the shore. He was going along. Across the water he saw them playing ball. Uh-oh, now how can he get across? He wanted to play ball with the others, too. (And he must have been so cute!)

A!... nomiyan wenil pemi-sukilicil.

Ah!... he saw someone paddling along in a canoe.

"Nathulin! Nkoti-li okamok. Nkoti-na nil naci-wici-epeskom. Ktakonutomulonc eltaqahk waht weciyay."

"Hey, come get me! I want to go to the other side. I want to go play ball with them, too. I'll tell you the news from where I've been."

Kehtol, 'tepehlan.

Pemiyahtit, 'tiyal yaq, "Nehe, akonutomuwin."

"Pol ehta nkotuwi-wtom."

Utoman. 'Pitsonsin. 'Posqolehtoman, utoman. Nemq-ote kisi-wtome, 'tiyal yaq, "Nehe, toqc ehta akonutomuwin."

"U, temonuk. Pol ehta nuliyan nutomakon." Kisi-woliyat utomakonol, elinaqahk sopoqikcahan sakhi-nutehewik. On 'totoli-woliyan, 'totoli-woliyan. Mam-ote yey, kisehlat. Nita.

"Nita, atkuhkewin weciyayin."

"Temonuk, pol ehta nuli-punan nutomakon."

Of course, he took him aboard.

As they were going along, he said to him, "Well then, tell me the stories."

"First I want to smoke."

He smoked. He filled his pipe. He lit it, and he smoked. He had hardly finished smoking, and the other fellow told him, "Well then, tell me the stories already."

"Oh, just a minute, I have to clean my pipe." When he cleaned his pipe, so much ugly tobacco residue came out. And he kept cleaning and cleaning. Finally he was done with it. Uh-oh.

"Well, then, tell me about your trip."

"Wait, I have to put my pipe away."

Mmm... mam-ote 'kisi-pisehlal 'pitsonakonok. (Nit-al 'qonatokosossin not.)	Mmm... finally he had put his pipe into his pocket. (It must have been about that short.)
'Kisi-pisehlan.	He had put it in.
"Nehe, akonutomuwin toqca." On yey kis maceluwehe wot. "Kcuwahpahkallonc!" (Nokatomon cuwahpahkalan.)	"Well then, tell me the stories right now." And by then he was starting to get angry. "I'll throw you into the water!" (He was afraid of being thrown in.)
"I!... pol ehta nsoniqin, pol ehta nsoniqin."	"Eee!... first I need to blow my nose, I need to blow my nose."
On 'sakhi-nutehtun yut elalokittiyekok yut 'tahkosqep, wisokocoke, psi-al keq. 'Kisi-qeci-milan yut; ma-te wihqonomuwawon.	And he pulled out this horrible-looking handkerchief, very filthy, with all kinds of stuff. He tried to give it to the other fellow; he wouldn't take it.
Yet memhuwi-soniqit nekom, nit eli-soniqit, on wakaw 'tomiqessin. On ma-te kisacomiw. Ma-na kisi-epeskomew.	Then Eniqs blew his nose so hard, and when he blew his nose, the poor thing's head came off. And he couldn't tell the story. And he couldn't play ball, either.
Nit-te psiw. (On-al 'qosikiness!)	That's all. (And he must have been so ugly!)

Sikiliyem

Cricket

as told by **Elizabeth Lacoote** and **Wayne A. Newell**

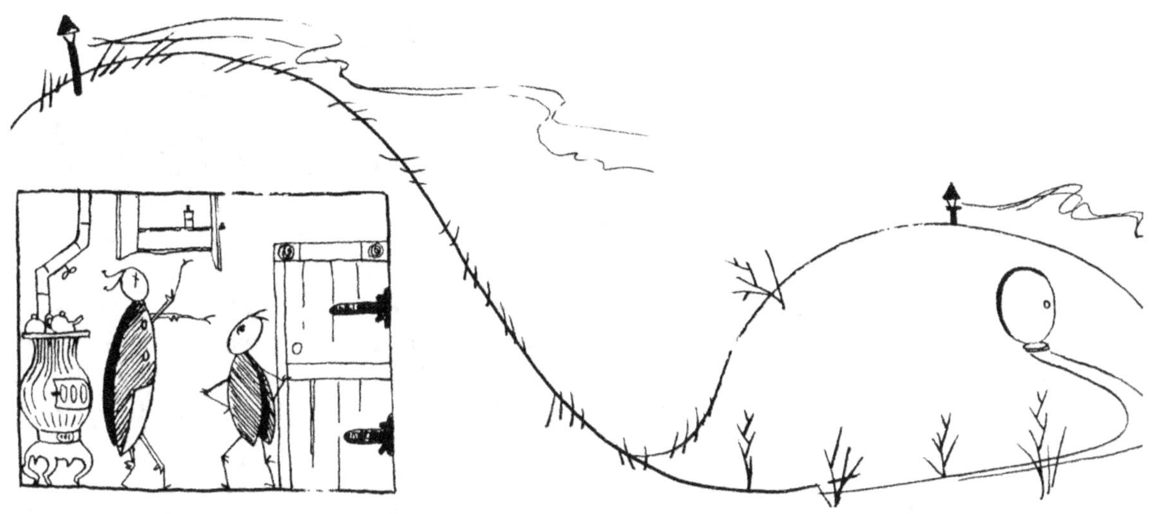

Ki! ... Wot yaq sikiliyem. Wikicik, naka 'qossisol. Komac yaq ktomakeyuwok. Ma yaq mitsiwiyik. Ma-te keq olluhkew, tehpu yali-pipiqe.... Aha.
A!... 'qossisol yaq 'tiyan wot sikiliyem, "Natcanomuwan knicaloq eli-mimehtayiq."

Gee! ... There was this cricket. He lived with his little son. They were very poor. They didn't eat. He didn't do anything, just went around playing his flute.... Yes.
Ah!... this cricket said to his son, "Go to your uncle and borrow some grease for our food."

A!... macahan skinuhsis. Mam-ote peciye nemaht, nicalkul eyilit, amushopihkiyil. Nita, 'tiyal yaq, "Ntatat yaq wocanomulihc eli-mimehtayek eli-mimehtayek."

Ah!... the boy went off. Finally he got there, where his uncle was, a spider. Uh-oh! He said to him, "My dad wants you to lend him some grease for our food – some grease for our food."

“Not ehta ktatat, kat-te keq oli-koluwosiw. Cel-ote ma ’poqahtuwon tan elihpiyeq. Kotama-na maqehtehmuwon micuwakon. ’Qoci-nipon-otehc yali-pipiqe. Eci-maleyit.”

“That father of yours, he isn’t worth anything. He doesn’t even earn enough for you to eat. And he doesn’t gather food. All summer long he goes around playing his flute. He’s so lazy.”

Olomi yaq qolopatopuwa. Amucaluwewi-wawikon yaq milan. “Yuta maceptuwan. Maceptuwan yut ktatat. Musa-te-na apc sakhi-ntutomuwihkoc. Nekom-ona luhkec, ehqi-yali-pipiqec.” Nita!

He turned around in his seat. He gave him a fly’s backbone. “Take this to him. Take this to your father. Don’t come in here begging again. Let him work, and stop playing his flute.” Uh-oh!

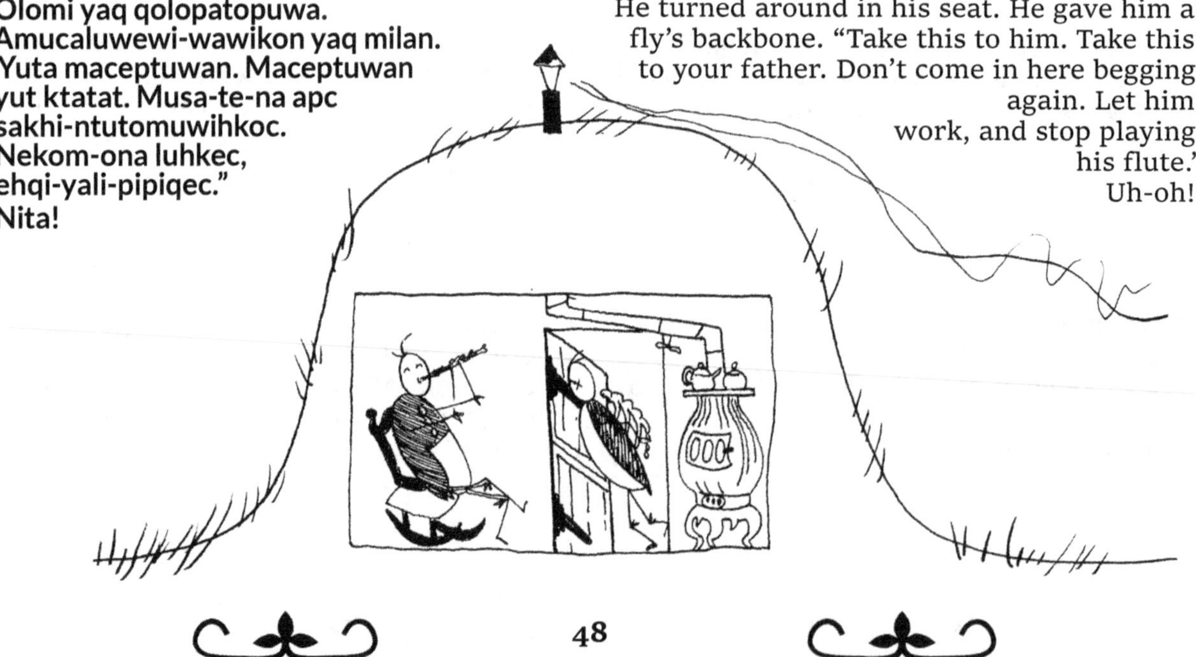

Sqotes naka Apiqsehsis — Spark and Mouse

as told by **John Nicholas**

Apiqsehsis naka sqotes pemkawoticik. Mam-ote 'petkawotiniya sipuhsis eyik. 'Tiyal yaq Sqotes Apiqsehsisol, "Tan-oc ktoli-kisi-qsokahkawotinen"?

A mouse and a spark were walking along. Finally they came to where a brook was. Spark said to Mouse, "How will we be able to get across?"

On yaq apiqsehsis naci-kotunotun pskihq naka 'kosokayahqi-punomon yut ihik sipuhsisok. 'Kosokayatuwahan Apiqsehsis, wot-olu Sqotes petatuwet epahsiw. 'Tiyal yaq, "I!... eci wolapekiyak yut! Yut-tehc ntotolapeki."

And Mouse, they say, went and picked a blade of grass and laid it across the brook. He scampered across quickly, but Spark only got to the middle. He said, "Eee... this swings wonderfully! This is where I'm going to swing."

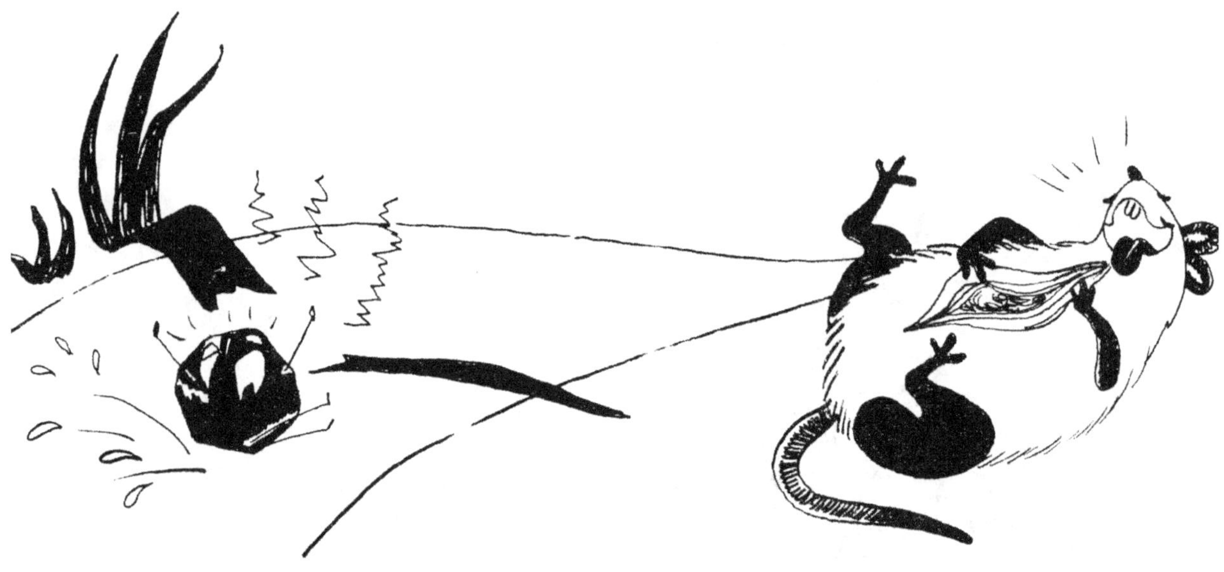

’Tiyal yaq wot Apiqsesis, “Kamot knattokassin! Temonuk knokkayaqosomon pskihq naka kcuwahpamin.”

Mouse told him, “You’d better get to the other bank! Otherwise you’ll burn up the grass and fall in.”

“Kat-op keq ntolessiw!” Sqotes itok.

“Nothing will happen to me!” said Spark.

**Kesq yaq wot Sqotes etolapekiyat, on tomaqote pskihqis, on ’cuwahpiyan. On cewahpiyat, on ’qasqomessin.
On Apiqsehsis ’siktelomin, etutelomit mam-ote paskesson iyey mikikon.**

While Spark was swinging, the blade of grass burned through, and he fell into the water. And when he fell in, he melted. And Mouse laughed. He laughed so hard that he split his chest open.

On macahan tama-al wikuwamok. On skitapiyil 'tiyal yaq, "Mec-op-al kwicuhkemi? Npaskess etutelomi."

And he went to a house somewhere. And he said to the man, "Can you please help me? I split my chest open laughing."

On 'kisi-kpukuwan piksi-piyehs ewehket. Nit weci-ksi-mimeyit apiqsehs yaq toke.

And he sewed him up with a hair from a pig. That's why mice are so greasy today.

Wahant
Devil Stories

Wahant — Devil Stories

as told by Irene Newell, Elizabeth Newell, and Lorraine Gabriel

Kihke Wahant — The Devil Plants a Garden
Nutapektuhusit — The Fiddler
Tolamotultuwok — The Card-players
Moci-ehpit — The Evil Woman
Witimiye Wahant — The Devil Goes to Church
Wisawi-maniyeyal Sopiqonol — Golden Tears
Suwahqihike — The Bell Rings
Papahtomuwewtimok — Praying
Etolispasultimok — At the Wake

Illustrations by Faye Hoban

Kihke Wahant

The Devil Plants a Garden

Wahant yaq not ma pahculuweskiw. Keqsey kisi-itok, cu 'tolluhkan ma 'tuwehkawon koluskuwakon.

Neqt yaq wot skitap kotuwokihke; elkihqahk kis kiskesasik yey ktahkomiq. Sesomitahasu wenil-op wicuhkemihcil ekihket. Nit-te yaq weci-wihqimat wahantuwol: wahantoluhkan.

The Devil, they say, does not cheat. Whatever he has said, he will do—he doesn't use lies.

One day, it is said, this man wanted to plant a garden; he had plowed a big plot of land. He wondered whom he could get to help him plant. And that's why he called on the Devil: to do devil's work.

A...'peciyan wahant. 'Tiyal yaq, "Mec-op-al kwicuhkemi ekihki? Epahsiwc kmillon kihkan kisikk."

Ah... the Devil arrived. The man said, "Can you please help me garden? I'll give you half of the crop when it's grown."

"Kehtol-al, aha, kwicuhkemol."

"Of course, yes, I will help you."

I... mahkiyewossis 'kihka-neqqenikiya, pocetesol kiskihkatomuhtit. Mam-ote yey pesqahsuwek nihtol, 'peciyan wahant, natsakihtun kihkan. I...eci-wolinaqahk pesqahsuweskil.

Eee... after a little while, he had finished all of the planting, potatoes it was that they planted. Finally, when the potatoes had blossomed, the Devil came to see the garden. Eee... the blossoms looked so nice.

'Tiyal yaq wot skicin, "Nehe, ktepahsonomapon. Keqsey peyemitahatomon, yut lamiw eyik kosona tehsahqiw eyik?"

The man said to him, "Well, we'll each take half. What do you prefer, the part that's underground or what's above the ground?"

Wahant eci-wolinok pesqahsuweskil. 'Tiyal yaq, "Tehsahqiw."

The Devil really liked the look of the flowers. He said, "Above the ground."

Mam-ote 'tiyal yaq wot skicin, "Nit tuciw kpeciyan." 'Kisi-nsotuhmuwan kisuhsol walkahtimok. Mam-ote walkasik pocetesol, 'peciyan wahant. Coqahk-al, yuhtol pocetesol skitap nokka-pkonomonol, on tehpu staksok wahant (ma-te pesqahsuweskil).

Finally, the man told him, "Then you come back when the time is right." He told him the month when they'd be digging. At last, when the potatoes had been dug up, the Devil arrived. Of course, the man picked all the potatoes, and the Devil got only these stalks (there weren't any flowers anymore).

Ma-te keq itomu. Ma kisi-itomu, "Kpahculi." Nit-te eli-kishomawotihtitpon.

He didn't say anything; he couldn't say, "You cheated me." That was the deal they had made.

Mam-ote apc elikotok wihqiman, 'Tiyal yaq, "Yey, mec-op-al apc kisi-wicuhkemi? Ktepahsonomaponc."

Eventually, the next year, the man called him once more. He said, "Umm... can you please help me again?"

On 'tokihkatomoniya iyil masqositol, elinaqahk yaq masqositol. Mam-ote apc pesqahsuwek eci-wolinaqahk, 'peciyan wahant, natsakihtun kihkan.

And they planted beans, a lot of beans. Finally, when they had pretty blossoms, the Devil came to see the garden.

'Tiyal yaq skicin, "Keqsey peyemitahatomon, lamiw eyik kosona tehsahqiw eyik?"

The man said to him, "Which do you prefer, the part that's underground or what's above the ground?"

'Tiyal yaq, "Tokec kahk ma kisi-npakotuwiw, tokec kahk lamiw eyik."

The Devil said, "You can't fool me now. This time I want what's underground."

Coqahk-al, kisikok masqositol skitap 'kotunotun. Yat-olu tehpu wocopskiyil. Wocopskiyil yali-kotunotahsit. Nisokehs 'kisi-npakotuwal.

Of course, when the beans were ripe, the man picked them. The other one got just the roots. He went around picking the roots. The man had fooled him twice.

Nutapektuhusit

The Fiddler

Nit-ehta pihce Motahkomikuk, ehtahs-ote yaq piskolaqiyak, kissakhiyat nutapektuhusit, cel pihtahqekiye 'topsqons. Tan etuci-maciyapektuhusit, psi yaq-ote wen wonakessu naka 'pomokan.

Once a long time ago at Peter Dana Point, each evening a fiddler would show up, and he had a long overcoat. Whenever he began to play, everyone would get up and dance.

Wot yaq-olu skinuhsis nit 'topin naka uhkomossol, kosona-al wenil, mamamol. On 'kisi-yahan mamamol, 'tiyal yaq, "Mam, not nutapektuhusit pesqon ptoqakin 'qat."

This boy was sitting there with his grandmother, or someone, maybe his mother. And he said to his mother, he said, "Mom, one of that fiddler's feet is round."

Not yaq-olu nutapektuhusit, cu-al-lu 'kosicihtun etoli-tpolumiht. Tehpu 'topsqons tett qeni-oloqehtaq, 'toli-qeci-katun nit 'qat. Ipa, yuktok nit-te nutehkawotiniya.

Ipa, wot ehpit 'tiyalacomin yuhuht ihi witapiyi. 'Takonutomuwan, cu-al-lu spasuwiw. 'Tiya yaq, "Ptoqakin 'qat not nutapektuhusit."

Ma yaq-ote wolamsotuwawiwal. Apc welaqiwik, nahaht-ote piskolaqiyak, kis apc pessehtek ihtoli-maqahamok, apc etolokacik. Apc-ote peciye not, totolapektuhusu. Etolokawolotihtit. Etolokawolotihtit, mam-otehc cehqot.

Mam-ote wot-olu ehpit nisuwihticil piskiyak 'toliyalin, naka naci-kikimapin possiyanteskik. Yukk tahk yaq psi-te pokahkonihputetul 'qatuwal, neketok 'pomokaniya. Etuci yaq wolihtaqahk. Ipa, not skitap uci-macahan. Mam-ote apc piliwoss 'toliyan, 'tapi-tuwapin. Tehpu yaq etolokahtit athusossuwok, nikk-olu sissihqiyik. Athusossuwiyawolotukk. Etuttehkomuhtit, etolokawolotihtit.

Ipa, on pahtoliyasol 'kinuwehtuwaniya. Peskuhuk 'tolapasiniya, peskuhuk katama. On pahtoliyas 'kispekehtun imiyewp ewehket. Ktasson ihtoli-maqahamok.

Cel yaq kakehsukoniw ahtoli-sakhi-pkotete nit ktahkomiq. Cel yaq mete-masqolamultihtit elomi-motekawolotihtit, elomi-kcitassultihtit.

But for sure that fiddler knew they were talking about him. He just moved his coat like that, trying to hide that foot. Well, the boy and his mother walked out.

Now the woman went around telling the story to her friends. She probably told them about it the next morning. She said, "That fiddler's foot is round."

They didn't believe her. The next night, as soon as it began to get dark, and the hall was lit up again, they were dancing again. He came again, and he was fiddling. They were dancing. They were dancing until dawn.

But finally, that night, this woman's husband went there, and he went to peek in at the window. All of their feet were chafed raw and bloody, but still they danced. The music sounded so good. Well, that man went away from there. But soon he went again, to look in. There were only snakes dancing, rattlesnakes. They had all turned into snakes. They were dancing so hard, dancing and dancing.

Well, they told the priest about it. Some people went there, some didn't. And the priest sprinkled the place with holy water. The dance hall sank into the ground.

And for many days, they say, smoke came out of the ground there. And they could be heard screaming as they went on dancing and sinking deeper and deeper.

Tolamotultuwok

The Card Players

Neqt kete nil nikonuk, Motahkomikuk, ntapsokiluhpon, kenoq-olu nuspas. Nit-te piskiyak, 'petapasiniya skitapiyik on 'tamotultiniya tolehp.

One time, for example, at our house, at Peter Dana Point, I was small, but I was still awake. When it got dark, some men came to play cards.

Niponiw apqotehte khakon.

In summer the door was open.

Mam-ote nit wiwonikuwok-otehc tuwihputik etolamotultihtit. Neqt etolamotultihtit, komotu sakhi-ksahat olomuss, mokoseweyu olomuss elkilok. Woli-te olomi-pisuhsiya lami-neqi-tuwihputik.

Finally, they were crowded tightly around the table playing cards. Once when they were playing, all of a sudden a dog came in, a big black dog. He went right in under the table.

Yukk-olu 'siktehpawolokuwal-ote skitapiyik etolamotultitponik. Nit-te epultihtit, tehpu 'tassokinuwawal. Kisi-wiwonuhset nit lamiw, apc 'tolomi-nutewsan. On wen-al unakessin naka naci-tuwapin khakonok.

But he frightened the men who were playing cards. They just sat there staring at him. He walked around underneath, and then he walked out again. And someone got up and went to look out the door.

Ma-te tama ihiw. Nit-te etoli-ksihkassit.

The dog wasn't anywhere to be seen. He had disappeared.

Moci-ehpit

The Evil Woman

Yut-ehta wikicik ehpit naka skitap, wasisuwiwok. Eci-woli-nisi-ihihtit. Ma kolultiwiyik, woli-pomawsuwinuwok, etucitahamtihtit. On wahant, ’totoli-qeci-coceponan, ’toli-pawatomuwan matonotilin.

A man and a woman lived here who were very young. They were a wonderful couple. They didn’t argue, they lived well, they loved each other very much. And the Devil, he was trying to separate them, he was wanting them to fight with each other.

Nama, ehtahs-ote sontek witimiyik toqi-te, kuhpehsewiwok. Eci-ehta woli-pomawsuwinuwihtit. ’Taluwi-te wahant cocepehla.

No, every Sunday they both went to church, and they confessed. They lived such good lives. The Devil couldn’t separate them.

On mihqitahasin yuhtol ehpilicil wikilit, moci-ehpit. 'Qotuhkanu, nit wiku qihiw.

And he remembered this woman who lived there, an evil woman. She lived alone, nearby.

'Tiyal yaq yuhtol ehpilicil, "Mec-op-al kwicuhkemi? Ptoqapossis-oc kmillon wisawi-man."

He said to this woman, "Can you please help me? I'll give you a little sack of gold."

'Tiyal yaq ehpit, "Keq-op ntahcuwi-oluhk?

The woman said to him, "What would I have to do?"

'Tiyal yaq "Tokec kisi-cocepehlot niktok yut wikicik, tokec kisi-coceponot, nit-te kmillon wisawi-man."

He said, "If you can separate those two who live here, if you can separate them, then I will give you the gold."

Nit-ehta-te wot moci-ehpit nit-te 'tolluhkan. Amsqahs-ote yuhtol skitapiyil nemiyat, mocakonutomuwal: "Knisuwiyeq nit kisi-olluhket, kisi-tpinuwa piluweya skitapiyi." Yehtol-ona ehpilicil nemiyat, nihtol-ona 'tiyal, "Knisuwiyeq ehpilicihi 'tiyali-tpinuwa."

Well, then the evil woman did just that. The first time she saw the man, she told him bad things: "Your wife is looking at other men." And when she saw the woman, she also told her, "Your husband is going around looking at women."

Ipa, mam-ote 'kisehtuwan 'kolultilin nihiht. Elomi-kolultihtit, elomi-kolultihtit, mam-ote cocepiyyik. 'Kisi-cocepona. Yehtol-ote mocakonutomuwal, yehtol-ona.

Well, finally she made them argue with each other. They kept arguing and arguing, until finally they separated. She had separated them. She said bad things to the one, and also to the other.

Sesolahki-te yaq wahant sakhiyat, pihtahqot yaq opos sakhiptaq. Yut yaq qonasqiw ekhutek ptoqapossis, wisawi-man psonamkahte. Naka 'tolaqhomuwan yut opos nihtol ehpilicil. 'Tiyal yaq, "Na, yut wisawi-man kpeciptulon. Kil ktaqami-wahantu katok nil."

Then suddenly the Devil came in, bringing in a long pole. At the tip of it there hung a little sack, all full of gold. And he reached with the pole toward that woman. He said to her, "Here, I'm bringing you your gold. You're more of a devil than I am."

Ma yaq-ote wahant 'koti-wecuwawkuwawiyil, 'sami nokalal.

The Devil didn't want to get near her, because he was afraid of her.

Witimiye Wahant

The Devil Goes to Church

Yut yaq neqt etolimiyamok ehtahs sontek. Ehtahs sontek yaq-ote wot nutonahket nomiyal wenil imiyewikuwamok waht-ote ahasit weckuhqepilicil, cel pihtahqekiye yut 'topsqons. 'Kolonomon pilasq naka 'tiyalapin. Ehtahsi-mahkiyew-tehc yaq toluwikhike. Apc-oc 'tiyalapin, apc 'totoluwikhikan.

Once the people were attending mass every Sunday. Every Sunday, it is said, the altar boy would see someone in the church, sitting way in the back, and he had a long coat. He held a paper and looked around. Every once in a while he would write. Then he would look around again, and then be writing.

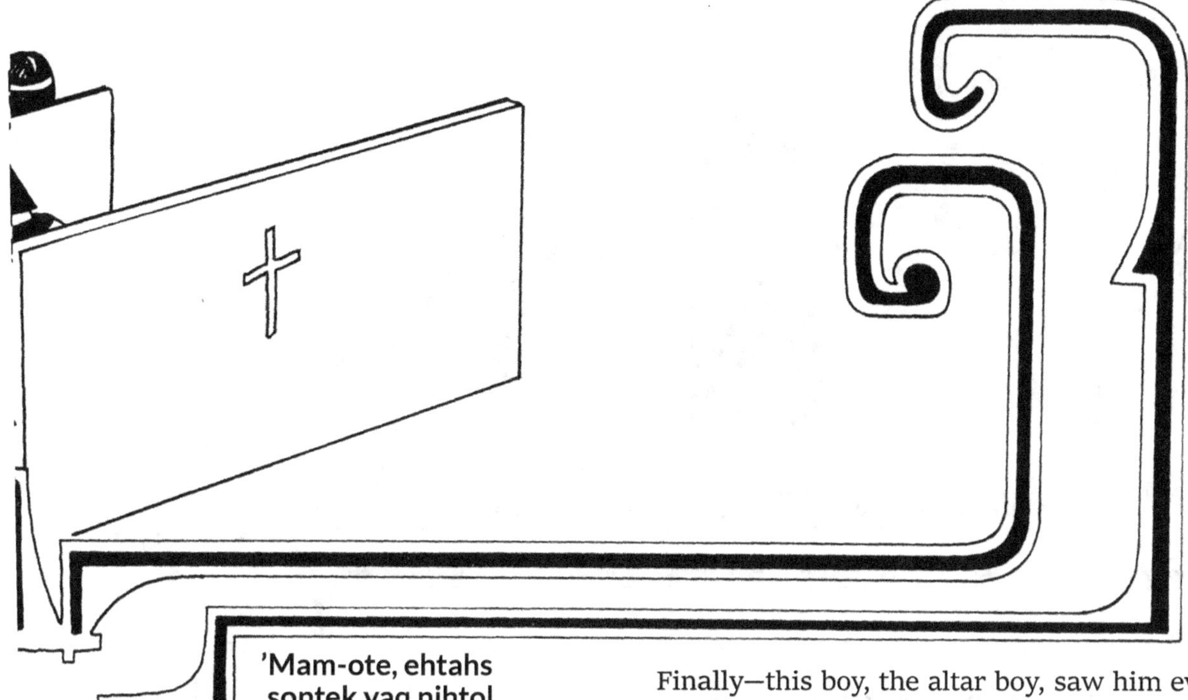

'Mam-ote, ehtahs sontek yaq nihtol nomiyal skinuhsis, wot nuci-nutonahket. Solahki-te pahtoliyasol 'takonutomuwan. 'Tiyal yaq, "Ehtahs sontek-ote yut nomiya wen ahasit pemqepit, upokkuthom, psi-te mokosewsewe wen." 'Tiyal yaq "Yalapu naka ehtahsi-mahkiyew-ote toluwikhike, apc-oc nita."

Finally—this boy, the altar boy, saw him every Sunday—one time he told the priest about it. He says to him, "Every Sunday I see someone here sitting in the back, with an overcoat on, someone dressed all in black." He tells him, "He looks around, and every so often he's writing, and then he does it again."

'Tiyal yaq wot pahtoliyas, "Knostuhmulon elluhkiyin apc nomiyot." 'Kisi-milan imiyakon. 'Tiyal yaq, "'Pahkamok kutkuwan tan etuci apc nomiyot, naka sesolahki-te knahsahkewan nihiht woniyakonok. Psi-tehc wen nomiyal." (Cu-al-lu pahtoliyas 'piluwitahamal.)

This priest said to him, "I'll tell you what to do next time you see him." He gave him a rosary. He told him, "Come up to him behind his back the next time you see him, and without warning throw this over his head. Then everyone will see him." (No doubt the priest suspected who he was.)

Woli-skinuhsis wot nuci-nutonahket, wisoki-woli-skinuhsisuwiw yaq.

The altar boy was a good boy, a very good boy, it is said.

Coqahk-al, apc ehsontek kis yaq wot etoluwikhiket, on wot skinuhsis ahasit utkuwan. Naka sesolahki-te yut nahsahkewan yuhuht imiyakon.

So of course, the next Sunday, this man is already there writing, and this boy comes up to him from behind. And suddenly he throws the rosary over his head.

Coqahk-al, ma-te kisi-macessiw, nit-te epit. Nasopu imiyakon 'qotakonok. Psi-te wen nomiyal. Elapultihtit pomawsuwinuwok, on pahtoliyas 'toliyan.

Of course, he can't move, he just sits there. The rosary is around his throat. Everyone sees him. The people look, and the priest goes up to him.

'Tiyal yaq, "Keqsey yut kil ktolluhk? Mehsi yut kil ksahayin ntimiyewikuwamok nil?"

He says to him, "What are you doing here? Why do you come in here, into my church?"

'Tiyal yaq, pahtoliyas, "Nil-ote-lu etololuhkewicik."

The man tells him, "These are my people who are working for me. They don't work for you."

'Tiyal yaq, "Katama, nil ntoluhkewkuk."

The priest says to him, "These people are working for me."

'Tiyal yaq, "Kikimuwasultuwok, kosona siktelomultuwok. Malikikemultuwok, yalapehpusultuwok. Psi-te wisuwonuwal ntihmuwanol."

He says to him, "No, they work for me." He says to him, "They whisper, or they laugh. They make fun of people, they keep looking around this way and that. I have all their names."

'Tiyal yaq pahtoliyas, "Katama, nil nikk eluhkewicik."

The priest says to him, "No, those people work for me."

'Totoli-cikawimtiniya mahkiyew, on pahtoliyas 'tolokiman yuhtol skinuhsisol naciptulin imiyewp. Naka pahtoliyas 'kisokitomon wikhikonossis. Kisokitok wikhikonossis, naka 'tolpekehtuwan nit imiyewp. Olomi yaq kcitassuwa, cel yaq sakhessik sqot, naka tuwalokessu-te pemsokhas. Kenoq nit apc wesuwehtehson pemsokhas.

They are arguing for a while, and then the priest tells the boy to go get some holy water. And the priest read from a little book. When he had read from the little book, he sprinkled the man with that holy water. The man sank away, it is said, and they say that fire came out, and that a hole appeared in the church floor. But then the floor snapped shut again, the way it had been before.

Wisawi-maniyeyal Sopiqonol

Golden Tears

Wotta yaq pihce ehpit, on mehcinan. Mehcinet on ehta 'cocahkumol macahalin spomkik. Nit yaq 'taselimol eyilit naka tuciw wahant. Cel yaq 'tihiniya tpapekhikon.

There was once this woman, they say, and she died. And when she died, her soul went to heaven. Her angel was there and also the Devil. And they had a scale.

I... etutuwulet yaq-ote wahant pilaskul, kehsi-milluhkets wot ehpit qeni-pomawsit. Wot yaq-olu wot ehpit 'taselimol kehsossok yaq nekom 'tahtuwikhikonol; 'tepehtun yut tpapekhikonok. Wahant etutuwulet-ote wikhikonol tepehtaq. Coqahk-al, cel yaq yehtol ewephutuwat kehsi-wolluhkets.

Eee... the Devil had such a big load of papers, all the different things the woman must have done while she was alive. Her angel had only a few papers to put onto the scale. The Devil loaded on so many papers, filling it. Of course, the side of the scale with all her good deeds went up.

'Tiyal yaq wahant, "Nil wot ntopeloma."

The Devil told the angel, "I own this one."

'Tiyal yaq wot asel, "Mesqa."

The angel said, "Not yet."

Yut yaq-ote tama uci-muskehtunol sopiqonol, wisawi-maniyeyal. 'Tepehtun. Tepehtaq, on wahant ewephuke 'tahtuwikhikonol, eci-tkiqahk nihtol.

Then from somewhere he took out some tears, golden ones. He put them on the scale. When he put them on, the Devil's papers went up, the tears were so heavy.

Ipa, nekom 'topeloman. Weci yaq nihtol sopiqonol—anqoc yaq wen qeni-pomawsit, naka wen mihkuhman, nit-tehc yaq wen 'sasotemin, kosona moskeyin keq kisi-olluhket, on 'sasotemin, on-oc wisawi-maniyesson sopiqonol.

Well, she belonged to the angel. Because those tears—sometimes while one is alive, and one is reminded about what one did, then one weeps, or one is sorry for what one did, and one weeps, and then the tears turn to gold.

Suwahqihike

The Bell Rings

Wot pihce pesq skicin wikossomu. Nit tehpu yaq elluhket, ’kotuhsomin. Mam-ote ketuwahsonotek, on uli-punomon ’puktewickum. ’Keki-te sontek ma ’kiseltomuwawon nican wenil ’cipokihtaqsin kosona mihqotanis wen uskuweyutomon. ’Kekiw-ote ’qossihtun sonte. Nit-te-na nican elokehkimat.

There was once a certain man who drank a lot. That’s all he did: drink. Finally, on Saturday, he put his liquor away. All day Sunday he didn’t let any of his children make any loud noise nor anyone use a knife. All day he observed the Sabbath. And that’s also what he taught his children.

Nit kissontek, nit-te apc ’kotuhsomin.

Then on Monday, he drank again.

Mam-ote ’kosinuhkan on mehcinan. Pahtoliyas ma monuwehkahawiyil: kotuhsomuwin. Itom yaq, “’Sami-wikossomu. Elomocokek tama naci-puskonuk.”

Finally he got sick and died. The priest didn’t take him in: he was a drunk. He said, “He drank too much. Go bury him somewhere in the bog.

Coqahk-al tama-al elomi-waleyik naci-puskonaniya. Tahalu moci-pomawsuwin: tehpu olluhke kotuhsomu.

Of course they went and buried him in some hollow. Like a bad person: all he did was drink.

Wot-olu pahtoliyas, elomi-tpuhkiwik, komotu yaq metehtaqahk suwahqihikon imiyewikuwamok. On ’tamihkin, ’toliyan, wot-tahk yaq... not skicin mehcinetpon.

This priest, during the night, all of a sudden heard the bell sounding in the church. And he got up, went there, and there stood this... that man who had died.

’Tiyal yaq yuhtol pahtoliyasol, “Npawatomon knaci-ketalkehlin naka ktepehlin puskonikonihkuk.” ’Tiyal yaq, “Keluwosit nil nunheltomaq. Weci-unheltomuwit eli-qsihtuwanpon sonte.”

He said to the priest, “I want you to go dig me up and put me in the graveyard.” He said, “God forgives me. The reason he forgives me is that I observed the Sabbath.”

Nit-ehta-te yaq pahtoliyas ’suwahqihikan, woli-te. Skicinuwok nutomuhtit elomi-tpuhkiwik suwahqihikon, ’toli-qaskultiniya, tan li-tpiye. On yaq pahtoliyas ’tacomin.

The priest rang the bell right away. When the people heard the bell in the middle of the night, they went running to see what was happening. And the priest told them the story.

’Tiya yaq, “Woli-te knaci-ketalkehlaniya notta, naka ktepi-iywaniya puskonikonihkuk.” Ksepha ehta-te imiyewikuwamok, on yaka tuciw iywan.

He said to them, “Go immediately and dig him up and put him within the graveyard.” He was brought right into the church and there he was given a proper funeral.

Papahtomuwewtimok

Praying for One Another

Skicinuwok eliwihtomuhtit papahtomuwewtimok. Pihce Motahkomikuk imiyan tpuhk, skicinuwok, ma-te pahtoliyas. Skicinuwimiyan, 'tolintuhtiniya. On-oc tan etuci ciktek imiyewikuwam, komotu-te metiyapqotessik khakon. Mote-ksahan wen, mote-wolopin wen. Ma-tehc-olu wenil nomiyawiwal. Apc-oc wen mote-wonakessin, mote-nutahan. Kosona apc wen mote-ksahan.

The people call it praying for one another. A long time ago at Peter Dana Point, there were prayers at night, just the people, no priest. It was prayer in Passamaquoddy, and they sang. And when the church was quiet, all of a sudden the door could be heard opening. Someone was heard coming in and sitting down. But they didn't see anyone. Then, someone was heard standing up and going out. Or someone else was heard coming in.

Nit ehta itomuk, ma yaq wen ciksotuwawi puwinu tan etuci-papahtomuwewtimok.

But they would say that one does not listen to dead people when prayers are being offered for them.

On yaq wot pesq skitap pihce ma ulamsotomuwon. Mam-ote tpuhk elitahasit yaq, coke 'toliyan puskonikonihkuk, 'tantimol elossinolit, naci-ciksotomon. Naci-ciksotuwan nihtol, eltaqahk yaq, eci-miltaqahk psi keq nutok.

And this one man at that time didn't believe it. Finally, at night, he thought, why doesn't he go to the graveyard, where his aunt is buried, and go listen. He went to listen to her, and there was a lot of noise, all different noises that he heard.

Mete-masqolamit, metemiyat, mete-wisokatuwet. Naka keqsey yaq 'tiyukul, ma-tahk nostuhmuwon keqsey 'tiyukul. Eci kenuk yaq ktomaktaqahk.

He heard her screaming, praying, swearing. And she was telling him something, but he didn't understand what she was telling him. But it sounded so pitiful.

Ipa, not skitap elomi-tpitahasit, elomi-tpitahasit, mam-ote wonatomine. Ma-na 'kisiwihtomuwon nit, 'sami kisi-yahan kat-op wenil 'tiyawon. Kat-oc 'tacomiwon.

Well, that man kept thinking about it and thinking about it, and finally he went crazy. He couldn't say it, because he'd been told not to tell anyone. Not to tell the story.

Cu-al-lu lamkik iyu not ehpit, eci-ktomaktaqsit.

That woman sounded so pitiful, she must have been in hell.

Etoli-spasultimok

At the Wake

Pihce, anqoc wen minuwawsu. Wot kete wen-al skitap, stehpal amuwiyahsit, mehcinelit, on 'kacitahamaniya. On woli-te 'cossokhikonahaniya. Wespasultimok, ma apqotepiw. 'Cipitahamawal yaq.

Long ago, sometimes a person would come back to life. For instance, this one man, who was a little crazy, when he died, they wanted to get him out of sight, out of mind. And so they nailed his casket up right away. At the wake, his casket was not open. People were afraid of him.

Elomi-tpuhkiwik komotu metehtihiket. On yaq macephulhotiniya peskuhuk. Yukk-olu qocomok eyulticik ksiyapasuwok naci-wewisultiniya, yektok-olu kotokik nutephulhotuwok. Nit etoli-cocuwawotultihtit khakonok.

During the night, suddenly he was heard knocking. And some people ran away. Those who were outside went in to see what was going on, and those others were running out. They got all snarled up with one another in the doorway.

Ipa, on wen-al skicin pesq, 'tiyaliptun possaqhenomakon, alahsenoma.

Well, one of them was carrying a lantern, shining it around.

'Tiya yaq, "Apc tan?"

He said to them, "Now what?"

Itomuk yaq, "Motehtihike not."

They said, "He's knocking."

On yaq 'tapqotekuwan nekom. Cel yaq ktoqossin, elinaqahk pokahkon sakhiyewik. Tuhkiyat, cu-al-lu pskikitessu. Litahasu kis lamkomiq iyu.

And they pried open his casket. And he was lying there face down, with a lot of blood coming out. When he woke up, he must have died from terror. He thought he was already underground.

Kehtaqs

Ghost Stories

Kehtaqs — Ghost Stories

as told by Irene Newell

transcribed by Mary Ellen Stevens Socobasin

illustrations by Roger Gabriel

Antiw – Auntie (My Late Aunt)

Ktopinaq Wahant – The Devil Is Watching You

Kehtaqsuwok – Ghosts

Motewolon – The Motewolon (person with extraordinary spiritual powers)

Kepcicuwok – At the Narrows

Sqotewi-ahahs – The Fiery Horse

Ehpit naka Puwin – The Woman and the Corpse

Antiw

Auntie

Antiw

Motahkomikuk kete mecimiw eci psi-keq mili-nomihtuhtihtit. 'Sami pihce ktanaqsuponik motewolonuwok. Nikk nit ellukhotihtit. Tan-ote keq wenil yahahtit, nit-tehc eleyik.

Nakaw kete 'toliwiyaponil Mali Miyawinaw. Asseloma ehta mamamkol nit eli-amalhiwiyahtit. Not kete eci-ptewolonuwit. Ntantim kete nit weci-mamatuwikokpon wolukon, eltehsit tehpu Antiw eli-pileyawilit 'payisihkolumol. Pemi pokomilit, Antiw keq al wetelomit. Nit te yaq 'toli lapoman.

'Tiyal yaq, "Ehqi yalelomuhkas. Temonu tama ktotoli ksinuhk."

Nemq yaq-ote not mehtewestu, on yaq tan-al 'tolessilin 'payisihkolumol, on Antiw 'kipiyan. On tan-al 'tolihtestun wolukon.

Tan-ote keq wenil ptewolon yahat, nit-tehc wen elessit.

Auntie

At Peter Dana Point, you know, it used to be that people saw a lot of strange things—because there used to be a lot of motewolonuwok (people with extraordinary powers). They're the ones that made these things happen. Whenever they told someone that something was going to happen, it would.

There was one they called Mary Miyawinaw. Sam's mother, that was her nickname. She was one of those motewolonuwok, and she was the cause of my aunt's hip getting crippled. It happened when Auntie got a new bike. She was riding along once, when she laughed to herself about something.

That Mary Miyawinaw was watching her.

"You stop smiling that way—or you'll get hurt!"

She had hardly stopped talking when something happened to the bike, and Auntie fell. She hurt her hip somehow. Whatever a motewolon tells you—that's what happens to you.

Ktopinaq Wahant

The Devil Is Watching You

Neqt yaq etolamotultihtit tehc yut wikit kosqehsuhs. Nit yaq ehtahs nipayiw, ’qoci-tpuhk yaq tehc.

There used to be an old lady living here. People played cards at her house every night—all night long.

Cel Mali San wasisuwiwuhpon. Kolamuwan yaq nit naci-witamkan. Kenoq-olu ehtahs-ote piskiyak, nit-te 'totolamo tultiniya, peci-te wasisok.

Mary Jane was a little girl then, and she was forbidden to go play cards. But every night there she was—and other children were there, too.

On yaq yut neqt etolamotultihtit, itom Walisossis, "Cess-tehp wen ihit. Ipa yet lap, possiyanteskik!" Itom, "Yet elapi, wot tahk wen elikit sakhapit."

One time when they were playing, Wallace said, "I feel as if there's someone here. Oh, look—there—in the window!" He said later, "When I looked there, someone ugly was peering in."

Sesomitahamahtit yaq tan 'tolessilin, naka yaq eci-wapkikit. Eluwe-te 'siktehpawolokul nihtol wenil. On ehta 'tolapawolaniya, tokkiw weli-enuwiyat. On 'kis akonutomuwan eli nit wen sakhapit elikit. Eluwe yaq siktehpayultuwok. 'Kihka yaq-ote macephuwolotuwok.

They all wondered what had happened to Wallace, he was so pale. Something frightened him almost to death. They splashed water on his face until he came to. And he told them what he had seen. They were so scared that every one of them ran out.

Ipa, Mali San nit uci-nuhsuhkakun wenil. Not-te-na nit elikit. Sehpal yaq etolahtuwek 'siskul naka 'tun. Yut yaq-ote ahasit weckuwi-mote-polahsit. Nit yaq-ote weci-macephoqaliht. Nemq yaq-ote kisi-ksetkuhu wikuwak, nit yaq-ote-na mote-cossotomhan.

Well, something chased after Mary Jane, something that looked just as Wallace had said. Its eyes and mouth were shining. She could hear it shuffling along behind her. I guess it chased her all the way home. Just after she got in the house, she heard it skidding to a stop outside the door.

Nekom yaq woli-te 'qociye yet wikuwossol elossinolit. Eluwe siktehpayu.

She went right over to her mother, who was in bed. Mary Jane was so frightened!

'Tiyukul yaq mamamol, "Mecimi-te kolamulon ktiyalamkan. Ma tahk kciksotomu." 'Tiyal, "Nit weci-nomiyot not wen. Kehtaqs notta."

"I always' told you not to go play cards," her mother told her. "But you wouldn't listen. That's why you saw that ghost."

Eluwe-te yaq-ona mosonokul.

And it almost got her.

Kehtaqsuwok

Ghosts

Neket kete yaq pemonahsit Nihkoloss. Itom, "Ahaci-te olomi-walaloke elomonahsi, cess-te wen sakolonomuwit nsuwhewik." Itom, "Ma-te sesomi-te nkisacqituwon."

You know, Nicholas was hauling firewood one time. He was going through Long Carry, he told me, when all of a sudden, he felt someone grab onto his pack sled. "I couldn't pull it, no matter how I tried," he said.

Itom yaq, "Toqc punalokittiyenomun nutapakon!" On yaq weke 'kosomahkewan wen 'suwhewik. Nuhkoskehtuhukun yaq-ote nit eli kehtaqs ksomahket suwhewik.

"So, I shouted, You let go of my sled right now! And someone pushed his pack sled right into him. It hit him in the back of the knees and he fell down."

Ma-te nit wen 'kisi-tuciyawon nipayiw, kosona wenil 'kosomahkanol kehtaqs. Tan-al-lu mec-al-ote pomawsu not kehtaqs. Cilomotasuhpon kahk.

You can't go there at night or that ghost will push you. I bet he's still living there. It was haunted for sure.

Yet-te-na toke Palinsis wikit aqamsoss, cilomotasuhpon. Ehtahs-ote nit wen tuciyat, cu wenil 'kisi-pkikalal. Neket itom Walis, "Cel kesalokittiyaltoqephit." 'Kisi yaq pkikatomakun 'tahsusuwon naka 'qasahkewkun.

And just beyond where Pauline lives now—that used to be haunted, too. Every time you went by there, someone would grab you. Once Wallace said it grabbed him by the hair so hard that it hurt. It took his hat off, too—and threw it away.

Tahalu-te-na yet kepcicuwok, nit-ona cilomotasuhpon. Ahcossis naka Henry Mahciw wenil 'kisi-nuhsuhkakuwaponil. Nit-olu tehsahqiw wen tuciye 'samaqanok, naka yaq eci-ciptaqsit naka 'cipinaqsin.

At the Narrows—that was haunted. Archie and Henry were followed by something. It could go right on top of the water, and it looked and sounded awful.

Nikuwoss-ona neqt 'toli-nomiyal wapeyilicil ahahsuwol qocomok, naka ma yaq-ote ahahs 'tihiwon skicinuwihkuk. Nihtol kete ma-te 'kosiciyawiwal tan-op wecessilit.

My mother once saw a white horse outside the house, and there weren't any horses on the Township. I mean, nobody knew where he could have come from.

Motewolon

Nikuwoss-ona neqt motewolonuwihponolahpon. Not-olu nikuwoss, ma-te 'kosicihtuwon eli-toli-motewolonuwihponolut.

Itom, "Neqt keti-kospahtahsi, ma ntiywaw kostokonikon. On naci-ntutomuwan wot Kci-Anuwit kostokonikonol, wot Johnson uhkomoskol." Waht yaq peciyat, 'tiyal yaq, "Ehpit, 'ci-milin kostokonikon."

'Tiyukul yaq, "Woli-te wicuhkems, wasis. Tehsahqtihikonok tama opu." Wot-olu yaq Kci-Anuwit, ma-te coni-posonutehkew.

Itom nikuwoss, "Apqotehtu tehsaqtihikon, wot tahk kikociw kelomit sipsis. Cel nit eli-lapomit naka 'siktelomin. Welapomuk, nonomuwan-ote not motewolon 'sisoq—Mali Pokomk not."

Elapit, nit-te-na qihiw ekhute cossakon. Tehpu yaq qeni-wihqonok, nit-te 'toli saptehmuwan 'sisoq. 'Siskuk yaq nit elonomtehsok, cel yaq nit elessit sipsis, elinaqahk yaq pokahkon.

On yaq nihtol wihqiman kosqehsuhsol, nakaw Kci Anuwit. 'Tiyukul yaq, "Not nit motewolonuwihponolosk."

The Motewolon

My mother was once cursed by a motewolon (person with extraordinary powers). But she didn't know that she was being cursed.

She told me that one time she was getting ready to wash the floors, and she was out of soap. So she went over to Old Hannah's house—that's Fred Tomah's grandmother—she's dead now. When she got there she said, "Woman, give me some soap."

"Just help yourself, child. It's in the cupboard somewhere." Old Hannah didn't even stop working on her basket.

Well, my mother said that when she opened the cupboard, she saw a bird, perched in the corner. And it looked at her and laughed! When she took a close look at it, she recognized the face of a motewolon—Mary Pokomk!

Right near the bird she caught sight of a nail hanging on a hook. So she just picked it up and stabbed that bird in the eye. The nail went into its eye and the bird fluttered. There was blood all over it.

My mother called for that old lady—Old Hannah—and the old lady told her, "That's a motewolon putting a curse on you."

Nit yaq-ote nikuwoss macahan, naka naci-kospahtahsin. Itom, "Nahaht-ote mace-kospahtahsi, komotu sakhi-ksewset Mali Pokomk."

After that, my mother went home to wash the floors. She'd no sooner started on them, when who should come through the door but Mary Pokomk!

'Tiyukul yaq, "Wasis, kpeci-kotuwapemol."

"Child," she said, "I've come to get your help."

'Tiyal yaq nikuwoss, "Nenhiyal kotuwapemi, naka eci-musqitahamiyin."

My mother was surprised. "And you want me to help you, even though you hate me."

'Tiyukul yaq, "Kil ehtahc tehpu kikihhin. Kisi nil motewolonuwihponolol."

"You're the only one that can heal me, because I've been putting a curse on you."

'Tiyal yaq nikuwoss, "Aha, nkosicihtun, 'sami knomihtulon-ote ksisoq." 'Tiyal, "Ma tahk nil ntihiw keq milol, ma-te 'pisun 'ciw ksisoq."

My mother said, "Yes, I know because I saw your face. But I don't have anything to give you, no eye medicine."

Itom yaq Mali Pokomk, "Keka-te nil paskesson nsisoq. Tan tehpu keq milin, muck-otehp 'samaqan. Tehpu kekesk sunhomuwin nsiskuk, nit-tehc kikihin."

Mary Pokomk pleaded, "My eye is almost bursting. Give me anything, even plain water. Just pour a little in my eye, and you'll make me better."

Wot nikuwoss eleyit, nit-te nihtol 'tahsihpilan. Nit yaq ote 'tiyukun, "Woliwon wasis. Kikihi. Kenoq kat-oc apc kotuwihponolu, tan-ote qenawsi."

The way my mother was, she did give her what she needed. "Thank you, child. You have cured me. I will never put a curse on you again as long as I live."

Ipa, nikuwoss eci-te woli-witapehkamat. Nikuwoss siki-mocikitsopon, nit-tehp nit nehpuhukun Mali Pokomk 'sisoq.

You know what? She became a friend of my mother's. If my mother had been really wicked, Mary Pokomk's eye would have killed her.

Pihce elinaqsit ptewolonuwok. Nit-te-na weci-kehsitpon kehtaqsuwok.

There used to be a lot of motewolons, that's why there were a lot of ghosts.

GABRIEL

Kepcicuwok

At The Narrows

Pihce, nisuwok skitapiyik tama-al tolluhkiyik. Waht tama-al elomakomek tolaqtihikiyik. On nit-te-lu ketuwahsonotekil, on-oc 'peciyaniya. Cel-oc apc spasuwiw wesuwessiniya.

A long time ago two men were working way off beyond Dana Point. They were cutting wood. On Saturdays they'd come home. Then the next morning they'd go back.

Ipa, neqt yaq yukk nisuwok weckuwyahtit, nit etoli-kuskawehtit. Naka mecimi-te nit 'toloqiyaniya, naka ma yaq-ote wocawsonu. Cu-al-lu 'kotqahkan wen.

Well, one time these two were on their way home when they capsized at the Narrows. And they always came through there. There wasn't even any wind. Someone must have tipped them over.

Ipa, wot pesq pskuwa. Nit tama 'toli-mskuwawal wecuwaw etoli-ktoqiyahtit. Not-olu kotok, ma-te pskuwaw.

Just one of them was found. They found his body near where the two of them had drowned. But they couldn't find the other one.

Ipa, on 'kisi-wihqimaniya nuci-komoqilicil. On 'komoqin nit qihiw etoli-kisi-kuskawehtit. Nemq-al-ote yaq kisi-komoku, nit-te apc wiqtokahkan ahpapiyil. Nit yaq-ote apc wihqapekhaniya. Eluwe-te yaq siktehpayu.

So they sent for a diver. They put him in where the two had capsized. He'd hardly gotten into the water when he tugged on the rope, and they pulled him back up. He was frightened almost to death.

Itom yaq, "Nil kat-op apc nit ntoli-komoqiwon, tan-ote kehsi-miliyeq man."

He said, "I'm not going down there again, no matter how much money you give me!"

GABRIEL

Eci yaq cipinaqsilit wenil nemiyacil. Sehpal yaq elomalokahtek nit kepcicuwok, nit tama-al lampeq, naka yaq eci-piskalokinaqahk. Nit yaq wen elikit sakhapit. Ipa, cu-al-lu not nokkahlal nihtol pucoqossinulicil, 'sami ma-te moskuwawiwal. Naka nit eci-cinitomehsok.

I guess he saw someone really terrible. There was a hole down on the bottom of the Narrows, and someone looked out of it at him. It must have eaten that other one who drowned. They never found his body even though the water there is shallow.

Mecimiw-ote nit wen ali-nomiyahpon. Kis yaq ktanaqsu nit kis etoli-ktoqessit, naka cinitomehsok.

Something used to be seen around there. Quite a few people tipped over there—where it's shallow.

Kehtaqs kahk psi-te tama kisi-yaliye, peci-te lampeq. Kenoq-olu kat not kehtaqs. Wen not piluwey.

A ghost can go anywhere—even under water. But that wasn't a ghost. No, that was something different.

Sqotewi-ahahs

Neke Lili wikihtit yut, nkisamotultinen. Kis-al-ote esqonatek aciye, nit etuci-wolossit Lili.

Ipa, on wot Henry Mahciw naka Sokas naka Ahcossis macephaniya Tiliyewol, toke nit Playstead wikit, nit wikihtitpon Makolit. Ipa, itom Henry, "Mace mawapasine. Macephane Tiliye."

Nil ntiya, "Kotama. Nil kahk ma nkoti-liyawon, possa nokatomon."

Itom Henry, "I . . . tan op al ktolessultinen, kehsiyiq?"

Ntiyan, "Kotama, kiluwaw-ote macephuk." Ipa, on ntiyan, "Pol nil macephiq." Eci-nokatom nikonuk tuhsan, ksi-piskalokahte.

On-oc nikuwoss nmotehtehmuwan possiyanteskik, ntapqotemakun. On yaka yukk maciyapasiniya.

The Fiery Horse

At the time that Lilly Gabriel lived here on the strip, we used to play cards. One night it was about nine o'clock and Lilly went to bed.

Henry and Philip and Archie were going to take Delia home. She lived over where Playstead's is now—that's where her mother, Margaret, used to live. Well, Henry said, "Let's all go together and take Delia home."

But I said, "No—I'm not going that way. I'm scared."

Henry said, "Eeee . . . what could happen? There are so many of us."

I told him, "No, you boys can take her." Then I said, "Take me home first." I didn't like to go into the shed at our house. It was so dark inside.

When we got there, I knocked at my mother's window, and she let me in. Then the others went on.

GABRIEL

Ipa, naka espaqahtek elomapasihtit. Nit ma-te wenil nomiyawiwal, kis yaka Tiliyewol api-macephahtit. On yaka wesuwiyapasihtit, wot yaq wen pemi-sakhiyat. Ansa yaq liku ahahs, cel yaq sakhamkolek 'tun naka 'siskul, peci-te wihton. Ahcossis nit-te yaq weci-kipiyat. Yukk-olu yaq kotokik weci-qolopotqihihtit.

They had to walk through very deep snow. They didn't see anyone until after they had dropped Delia off. Then, on their way back, something came into sight. It looked like a horse, with a fiery mouth and eyes—even its nose. Archie fell right down when he saw it. The other two took off in the other direction.

Itom Henry, "Mace-qasqiyek, Sokas elapit: ma-te Ahcossis." Itom, "Iya—wot tahk pemahqossit!"

Henry said that when they started to run, Philip looked back—no Archie. He said, "Uh-oh—there he is—on the ground!"

On yaq wesuwe-qasqin, 'pahkikalan, on yaq maciyacqiphan tokkiw apc yet Makolitk. Ipa, on Makolitol 'kisi-yahaniya.

He ran back and grabbed him and dragged him to Margaret's. They told her what had happened.

'Tiyukuwal yaq, "Yut-te ktoqonultiq."

She said, "You spend the night here."

'Tiyawal yaq, "Kotama, ntiyali-qiluwuhukeponc." Yukk-ona nokatomoniya tama 'kotqonultiniya.

But they told her, "No, our parents will be looking for us." They were afraid to spend the night away from home.

Nit weci-maciyalikonikhotihtit. Waht milawiw pqomik oloqapasuwok. Eluwe yaq neke siktehpayultuwok.

So they went off through the snow. Way out around on the ice they walked. They were just about scared to death.

Ipa, 'tanaqsuwok kisi-cilomotomuhtit nita. Elomiyak-ote ehqi-cilomotasuwe. Not kal-ona wen mehtahtuwiya.

A lot of people were bothered by ghosts there. But after a while it stopped being haunted. Whatever it was must have burned out.

Ehpit naka Puwin

The Woman and the Corpse

Yut yaq pihce skitap naka nisuwihticil waht-ote yaq kcihkuk wikuwok. Wot yaq skitap, eci-moci-skitapewit, kenoq yaq woli-ehpituwiwol nisuwihticil. Cel ehta uhsimisol pahtoliyasuwiwol.

Once long ago a man and his wife lived deep in the woods. He was a very wicked man, but his wife was a good woman. Also, her younger brother was a priest.

On wot skitap 'peci-ksinuhkan. On ehpit wiqtahan uhsimisol. Kenoq wot skitap mehcine mesq kisi-peciyahq pahtoliyas. Siki yaq mehcine, eli-moci-pomawsitpon. Ehpit yaq mace-wolehlan weci-kispekehlut naka 'punan kuhutik. Kenoq 'sipkaskuwyal uhsimisol, eli-wisokamoqessik.

The man became very sick, and his wife sent for her brother. Before he could get there, however, the man died. He died a very hard death, they say, because he had led such an evil life. The woman prepared him to be blessed with holy water, and she laid him out on the bed. But she waited a long time for her brother because of a very bad snowstorm.

Qenaskuwyat uhsimisol, komotuk eltaqahk metehtehsit puwin. On wot ehpit naci-wesuwe-punan elossinulitpon. Toke kahk cel 'kophomon khakon wesuwessit wahsiw. Mahkiyewoss wot apc metehtehsit puwin.

While she was waiting for him, all of a sudden her husband's body fell off the bed with a loud noise. She went in to put him back. And now she closed the door when she came into the other room. After a little while, though, she heard the body fall again.

Wahsiw eliyat ehpit, wot-tahk elossit epahsiw pemsokhasik. Ahaci-te 'tolomi-wecuwawkomon khakon not puwin. Yet eqeci-wesuwe-punat, wahka-te 'poqanal. Cel yaq toke ahaci-te olomi-tkiqol. Aha, wahka-te apc 'kisi-tehsahqehlal kuhutik.

When she went into the room, the body was lying in the middle of the floor, a little closer to the door than before. When she went to put him back, she could hardly lift him. He was heavier. Yes, she could hardly lift him onto the bed.

Nita, on yaq toke mace-cipomolsin. 'Kisi-kpasokahmon khakon, naka macemiyan. Nutiyapin possiyanteskik etolaskuwyat uhsimisol.

Now she began to be afraid. So she locked the door, and she began to pray as she watched at the window, waiting for her brother.

Komotuk-ote apc yaq metehtesit puwin, cel yaq aqami-tkiqtehsin tokec, naka ahaci-te olomi-wecuwawtaqot khakonok. Yet yaq elapqotehtaq khakon, wot-tahk yaq puwin elossit oloqiw khakonok; cel yaq apqotehtetul 'siskul. Naka yaq cel toli-macessu.

Suddenly, she heard the body fall again, and it sounded even heavier this time, and closer to the door. She opened the door. There was the body, lying nearby; and the eyes were open, and it was moving. She just slammed the door and locked it

Qeni tehpu kpotiyahket khakon naka apc 'koppasokahmon. Cel ehta wot puwin maciyapenike khakonok. On mace-tuwalokotomon khakon. Tomk yaq-ote pesqon 'pihtin 'kisi-saputehtun, apc yaq woniyakon, apc kotok 'pihtin.

again. The body began to scratch on the door. It started to gnaw a hole. First he put one hand through, then his head and his other hand.

Keka yaq kisi-saputessit, 'tiyal yaq nisuwihticil not puwin. "Kpeci-naciphul. Ma nil lamkik ntoliyaw 'qotuhkayiw."

When he had come almost all the way through, the man spoke to his wife, "I've come to get you. I will not go down to hell alone."

Keka-te nokka-saputiyalokotomon khakon, on ehpit nutomon suwahqihikonossisol weckuwihtaqahk. 'Kosiciyal yaq uhsimisol eli keka peciyalit. On yaq ehpit nute-qasqin naka natassihkuwan.

He had just about gnawed his way completely through the door when the woman heard the sound of little bells approaching. She knew that it was her brother, and she ran out to meet him.

Tokkiw-ehta peciyat pahtoliyas, kis 'kihka-apatawsuwa skitap. On wot pahtoliyas 'kispekehlan nihtol skitapiyil, cel ehta etuci yaq pkotesit kispekehlut. Eltaqsit yaq skitap masqolamit. Mam-ote apc mehcine.

By the time the priest got to the house, the man had come back to life completely. The priest sprinkled him with holy water, and it turned to steam where it fell on his body. The man cried aloud and finally he died again.

Ehpit etuci-wolitahasit. Cel yaq sasotemit etolimiyat. On mace-wiciyeman uhsimisol utenek. Ma-te apc nit 'toliyawon wikitpon.

The woman was very happy, and she cried as she prayed. She went away to town with her brother and never went back to her house again.

Nit nuhkomoss pihce elakonutomuwitpon nil apsokilan.

This is a story my grandmother told me when I was little.

Nit-te psiw.

That's all.

GABRIEL

Peskotomuhkati Atkuhkakonol

Passamaquoddy Stories

Peskotomuhkati Atkuhkakonol
Passamaquoddy Stories (19th Century)

as told by Lewis Mitchell

illustrations by Lee Suta

Note on Lewis Mitchell's Peskotomuhkati Atkuhkakonol: Passamaquoddy Stories

THE PESKOTOMUHKATI-ATKUHKAKONOL are traditional Wabanaki legends. These Passamaquoddy versions of the stories were told in the late 1800s by the Hon. Lewis Mitchell, of Pleasant Point, and published by John Dyneley Prince in 1921 as "Passamaquoddy Texts" in Volume X of the Publications of the American Ethnological Society. Because Mitchell's original manuscripts had been destroyed in a fire, the published text was an effort by both men to reconstruct the stories from memory. Consequently, there was in some places a strong English influence on the Passamaquoddy language in Prince's published versions. In the 1970s, through the efforts of many people at Motahkomikuk (Peter Dana Point, Indian Township) and at Sipayik (Pleasant Point), the stories were re-created from Mitchell's and Prince's written text and re-transcribed in the modern writing system.

In most places the language of the original was preserved, but in a few places grammatical and wording changes were made to conform to the spoken Passamaquoddy of the 1970s. A special effort was made to be sensitive to and to preserve the various methods and techniques used in the Algonquian storytelling tradition. A glossary of unfamiliar and little-used Passamaquoddy words will be found at the end of the legends. The word *motewolon*, which does not have a precise English equivalent, means "person with extraordinary powers."

Note that the names of many of the animal characters in these stories were given in Mi'kmaq in Mitchell's original texts; these have been changed to Passamaquoddy here. The English translation follows the Passamaquoddy text sentence by sentence. The intent is to reproduce accurately the meaning and style of the original language.

Wocawson

Wind

Skicinuwok wolamsotomoniyal kci-sipsol. 'Toliwiyawal Wocawson, nuci-putuwet. Tolawsu pihcetu lahtoqehsonuk, nit epit tehsahqiw kci-ponapskuk, mehtaluktek. Tan etuci-macilqenuwit, nit-tehc petson.

The Indians believe in a great bird. They call him Wocawson, the wind-maker. He lives far in the north; there he sits on top of a big rock where the clouds end. Whenever he moves his wings, the wind begins to blow.

Neket Koluskap mec yali-wiciyemat skitapiyi, puskiw na nekom mace-suku 'tulok, sipsuhke.

At that time when Koluskap still went around among men, often he, too, would go paddling in his canoe, hunting birds

Neqt neke ehtahsikiskahkil wocawson, wisokolamson. Ahaciw pomolamson, kospon-ote neke peciwehse naka petamoqessu. Kotama Koluskap kisi-yali-sukiw. 'Titomon, "Wocawson, wot kci-sips etolawsit lahtoqehsonuk, not nit elluhket."

Once long ago, the wind blew every day; it blew strongly. More and more the wind blew, until at last it gusted and brought on a storm. Koluskap could not travel about by canoe. He said, "Wocawson, this big bird who lives in the north, he is the one who is doing this."

'Qiluwahan. Komac pihcetu oliye, on yaka moskuwan. 'Totoli-mskuwal epilit kci-ponapskuk, wapeyu kci-sips.

He searches for him. He has to go very far before he finds him. He finds him sitting on a big rock—a huge white bird.

'Tiyan, "Muhsumi, kotama kotomakitahamawiyik qenossok?" Kil nit kisihtuwon mecokiskahk, wecawsok, eliwehsek. Kusami-macehlak kunoskiyik."

He says to him, "Grandfather, do you not have pity for your grandchildren? You are the one who has made the bad weather, the wind, the gusts. You move your wings too much."

Neketok kci-sips oli-ikotohom. "Yut ntihinehpon wisoki-nihkaniw. Pihce kiskul, mesq wen etolewestuhk, nil-ote amsqahs nutaqsiyanpon. Nil-ote-na amsqahs macehlukpon nunoskiyik. Mecimi-tehc-ona nmacehlak tan eli-wolitahatom."

In spite of this, the big bird continues yawning. "I was here at the very beginning. In distant days, before anyone spoke, I was the first one to be heard. I was the first to move my wings. And I will continue to move them as I please!"

Nit etuci Koluskap wonakessit. Etutsonit, petkil-ote aluhkihkuk. 'Toli-wihqehlal yuhtol kci-sipsol tahalu-tehp motehehsim. 'Kolonomuwan toqiw wonoski, naka 'poneqahkan eli-psikapskiyak nisonul kci-ponapskul. Nit-te-na etoli-nokolat.

At that point, Koluskap gets up. He is so powerful, he grows to the height of the clouds. He picks up this huge bird as if he were a duck. He holds him by both wings and throws him into a crack between two rocks. Then he leaves him.

Nit neke 'cimaciw, skicinuwok yaliyawolotuwok, 'kekiw tehc. Mecimi-woluwipon, kakehsukoniw, kakehs pemoluhkemkil naka kisuhsok, kospon-ote neke 'samaqan tukcokiyak. Etuci-paqtek, Koluskap kotama 'kisi-tahapiyatomuwon 'tul.

From that time on, the people could travel about, all day long. It was always calm—for days, weeks, and months—until at last the water became foamy from stagnation. So thick was it that Koluskap could not paddle his canoe.

On nit-te mihqitahaman kci-sipsol, on macahan, naci-nomiyan apc. Eli-te nokolatpon, nit-te apc eli-mskuwat, Wocawson ipocol askomawsu. 'Teweponan, 'punan apc ponapskuk, naka 'tapqehtuwan peskuwol wonoskiyil. Neke 'ci-maciw kotama tutolamsonihkew tahalu pihce.

And then he remembered the great bird: he set out; he went to see him again. He found him just as he had left him—for Wocawson lives forever. He lifted him up, put him back again on the rock, and opened one of his wings. From that time on, it was not quite as windy as long ago.

Koluskap naka Oqim

Koluskap and Loon

Pihce, waht tama qospemok Oktokomq, wikultwok skicinuwok—msi yaq-ote oqimuwok. Kisi yaq-ona skitapewehlosultuwok tan-te etuci-wolitahatomuhtit.

Long ago, far off on a lake in Newfoundland, dwelled some Indians—all they say, were loons. They could, it is said, change themselves into men whenever it pleased them.

Neqt pemkiskahk, Koluskap peciyat oqimuwi-utenek, komac kiwacinaqot. Kenoq-olu msi-te oqimuwok wolitahasultuwok nemiyahtit 'kihci-sakomamuwal. Kakehsukoniw mawe-putuwosiniya. Malom-ote Koluskap keti-macahat, on apc aqamok 'toqetokelhaniya.

One day, Koluskap arrives at the loon village—it looks very lonely. But all the loons are glad to see their great chief. For many days, they hold a great council together. At last, when Koluskap gets ready to leave, they try to get him to stay over for a longer time.

Nihikehs oqimuwi-sakom wiwonituwiye qospemok. Ehtaste 'cinituwiyemuhtuwal Koluskapiyil. Apcituwiyat-ote, 'tiyal, "Ktoluhkewolonen naka kwitapehkamolonen."

Three times the chief of the loons flies around the lake. Each time he passes, he dips his wings to Koluskap. As he is flying, he tells him, "Let us work for you and be your friends."

On Koluskap 'tasiteman, Kwitapehkamolc naka kpomawsuwinumok. Nil-ona ntoli-pawatomon kiluwaw kwitapehkaminiya. Ktoluwehkuhulpahc kotunkewinuwok naka kinuwehtahsuwinuwok.
Tokec ntahcuwi-wiwisa-natsakiyak kotokik npomawsuwinumok, supekuk qihiw wikulticik. Pawaliyeq, ktokehkimoloniyahc eli-wihqimiyeq."

And Koluskap answers him, "I shall be your friend and your people's. I, too, want you to be my friends. I shall use you for hunters and messengers. Now I must hurry away to visit others of my people, who live by the sea. If you want me, I shall teach you how to call me."

Koluskap 'kisokehkiman wihqintuwewakon, ansa oltaqot tahaluhp olomuss etolewehtaq. Kisi-nokolat, tan etuci wihqimahtit, 'kocicihtuniya eli-nutuwut. Mec-ote toke pemkiskahk, tan etuci skicinuwok nutuwahtit oqimuwol, itomuk, "'Toqimuhtuwal Koluskapiyil."

Koluskap taught them a calling song that sounds like the howling of a dog. After he leaves them, and they call him, they know they are heard. Even now, today when the people hear a loon, they say, "He is calling to Koluskap."

Koluskap naka 'Siwiyi

Koluskap & His Relatives

Koluskap neke wikuss monihkuk wiciw ktanaqsuwok skicinuwok, weyossisuwiwisultuwok—nit-te na elomahtuhtihtit—naka wiciw mociyehswok. Eluwe-te msiw 'tihiniya piluwitposuwakon. 'Kocoskuwalawal Koluskapiyil, on 'kisitahatomoniya nehpahaniya.

Long ago, Koluskap lived on island with many people who had animals' names—and that's the way they behaved—and with some partridges. Almost all had extraordinary power. They were all jealous of Koluskap and they decided to kill him.

Neqt Koluskap qeni-yali-piyaqtihikonihket, on 'komuci-macephaniya uhkomossol Muwinesqiyil naka uhsimisol Nimaqsuwehsuwol. Litahasultuwok, Koluskap 'kihka-nokolut monihkuk, cu mehcine, ipocol kotama 'kocicihtuwawoniya tan 'toli-piluwitposilin.

Once, while Koluskap was gathering firewood scraps, they secretly took away his grandmother Muwinesq, the she-bear, and his younger brother, Nimaqsuwehs, the sable. They thought that if Koluskap were left behind on the island, he would die, for they did not know of his extraordinary powers.

Apaciyat, uhkomossol Muwinesqiyil naka Nimaqsuwehsuwol komutonalakk. Maciyaphan sitomok sonuciw. 'Keskuhtehkuwal elomi-pusilicil Mociyehsuwol, kci-nacitahamtihticil, naka Koluskap 'siwiyi. Memhuwi-kakaluwama Koluskap, 'cipokihtaqsuwamal uhkomossol wesuwe-pcitahkewkun 'temis. On Muwinesq ulopehlan 'temis epahsiw altestakonok, tahalu-tehp skicinuwok etolahkehtit amkakon. Nit nahtokahtuhukuniya. Koluskap wihqehlan. Mociyehs, witapiyi, naka 'tahqnikon macahaniya Peskotomuhkatik naka Monahnuk.

When he returns, his grandmother Muwinesq and Nimaqsuwehs have been kidnapped. He begins trailing them along the water's edge. He comes upon Mociyehs, the partridge, his great enemy, pushing off with Koluskap's relatives. With a great cry, Koluskap calls to them; he shouts to his grandmother to send him back his dogs. And Muwinesq sets the dogs down in the middle of a wooden dish, using the same motion with which the people would toss dice in the traditional dice game. That motion carries them back to the shore. Koluskap picks them up.

Mahkiyewoss 'tiyultiniya, uci-pusultiniya. 'Qosokahawolotiniya Kespukitk. Nit-te mace-menakatkeniniya elomi-sonuceyik sopayiw Unamakik. Malom-ote peciyawolotuwok Oktokomq.

Mociyehs, his friends, and his prisoners set off for Passamaquoddy territory and Grand Manan. They stay there for a little while, then they leave. They go across to Yarmouth, Nova Scotia. Then slowly they make their way along the coast by way of Cape Breton. Finally they arrive in Newfoundland.

Koluskap atolahsimu oluwikonok kisuhsok wiciw 'temis. Totololahsimu weci-kisi-nuhsuhkuwat nacitahamcihi.

Koluskap rests for seven days, together with his dogs. He rests so that he can pursue his enemies.

Teponaskuhyak, macephan temis sitomok. Elomatqik 'tolapin. 'Tolintuwatomon motewolonuwintuwakon, wihqintuwama putepiyi. 'Peciman putepehsisol nutahcil, 'petoqotahan eyilit Koluskapiyil. Neket Koluskap natomokil. 'toqetpehkuwan, 'tolomelkin 'pahkamok on 'kottapehkuwan. Koluskap macekiman.

When the time has come, he takes his dogs to the shore. He gazes out over the waves. He sings a song of great power, luring the whales with his song. He attracts a little whale that hears him; he swims up to Koluskap. At that time, Koluskap was a man of great size. He tires to stand on him, he steps onto his back and sinks him. Koluskap sends him away.

Apc 'tolintun, 'peciman kci-putepiyil. Nihtol woli-kispehkuwal. 'qosokaphukun Kespukitk.

Again he sings, this time attracting a big whale. That one he can ride well. She carries him across to Yarmouth.

Malom-ote Putep nomiya 'sakehs lampeq. Komac wisoki-nokatomon etoli-apsitomek. Nokatomon 'cocokahtehsinon. Nit-te eli-pawatok Koluskap weci skat puskosonessihq. Keka nahtokassihtit, Putep 'toqecimulan. "Kis nomihtasu ktahkomiq?"

By and by, Putep, the whale, sees little lobsters in the water. She is very much afraid of shallow water. She is afraid that she will run aground. This is what Koluskap wants, so that he will not get his moccasins wet. When they have almost come across, Putep asks him, "Can land be seen yet?"

Nopakotuwal. 'Tiyan, "Kotama. Kat-olu ktahkomiq oli-kinuwehlosuwiw, tahalu tap elakiyat. Mec-ote pihcetu ktahkomiq iyu."

He does not tell her the truth. He tells her, "No, land announces itself, as you know, as the curve of a bow. The land is still far away."

On aqamok Putep 'taciyan.

And Putep continues on.

Ahaciw-olu olomi-apsitome. Nutuwa metentuhtilit ess lampeq. Lintuhtuwok, "Apoqahk naka kpiscopolan." Yuhuht ess op mehcinehloku. 'Kotunoloku. Putep-olu kotama nostuwawi.

However, it gets more and more shallow. She hears the clams singing in the water. They sing, "Throw him off and drown him." These clams would cut him to shreds. They are his enemies. Putep, however cannot make out what they are singing.

'Tiyan pemhulacil, "Keq-olu etolintuwatok ess?"

She says to her passenger, "What is the clam singing?"

'Toli-asitemal, "Wiwisay, wiwisay! Wiwisahulan tan-ote kisi-tuciyayin."

He answers her, "Hurry, hurry! Hurry him across as fast as you can go."

Nit Putep tuciye tahalu-tehp monomeqakon. Sesolahkiw 'cocokayessin. Nuhkonahtehsin, 'sikitahasu. 'Tolintun, "Nqenoss, knehpihi. Kat-op apc nkisi-monessiw."

Then Putep goes like lightning. Suddenly she runs aground. She hits softly on the shore; she is extremely worried. She sings, "My grandson, you are killing me. Never again can I get off from here."

Koluskap lintu, "Musa seksihkoc, uhkomi. Kat-op keq ktolessiw. Apc-otehc ktalhom supekuk."

Koluskap sings, "Do not fear, grandmother. Nothing shall happen to you. Again, indeed, shall you swim in the ocean water."

Koluskap nit-te 'toli-ksomehlal woniyakonok, ewehkahacil 'tahtapiyil. Nit-te Putep macehomon eli-koskitomek.

Then Koluskap pushes on her head, using his bow. So Putep swims out where it is deep.

Nit Putep mace-wolitahasin. Apc-olu wesuwessu, 'tiyukun. "Nqenoss, kotama ktiywaw ponapsqahson naka 'tomawey?"

Then Putep starts feeling happy. But she returns again, saying to him, "My grandson, don't you have a stone pipe and some tobacco?"

Milan utomakonol naka 'posqolehtomuwan. Putep wolitahasu. Maciyamahan, nspi-macetome. Koluskap sipkiw sankewikapuwu sonuciw, 'tapotukonapinol 'tahtapiyil. Nomihtun ciniye aluhk pemi-nuhsuhkaht Putep, tokkiw elomihkomapomut.

He gives her his pipe and lights it for her. Putep is pleased. She goes away, smoking as she swims. Koluskap stands still for a long time on the shore, leaning on his bow. He sees a low cloud following along after Putep until she can be seen no longer.

On apc Koluskap macephoqan, yali-qiluwahat 'siwiyi. Sipkiw pomiye, malom-ote peciye Oktokomq. Nipayiw oli-peciye, Nimaqsuwehs wikok. Nimaqsuwehs 'qotuhkanu. Macephan kcihkuk, 'kotunkaniya. Nit milan 'kospisun Nimaqsuwehsuwol: nit wici-milan-ona piluwapiyuwakon. Komac Nimaqsuwehs 'tawi-kotunke.

And again Koluskap sets off, searching for his relatives. He journeys for a long time; finally he arrives in Newfoundland. He arrives at night, at Nimaqsuwehs's house. Nimaqsuwehs lives alone. He takes him to the woods, where they hunt. There he gives his belt to Nimaqsuwehs, and with it his extraordinary power. Nimaqsuwehs becomes a good hunter.

Wespasahkiwik kahkakuhsusq nomiyal Nimaqsuwehsuwol etolipastulit wiyuhs wikok. Piluwitahasu. Nit-te nokosayiw psontaqot, msiw seksultin. Itomuk, "Kis wecuwawsu Koluskap." Msi-te wen ksephuwe wikok, 'taskuwahtun mehcinan.

In the morning, a female crow sees Nimaqsuwehs drying meat at his house. She becomes suspicious. Soon the word spreads all around—everyone is frightened. They say, "Koluskap is near." Everyone goes into his house to wait for death.

Yet messuwessit Koluskap, nomiya eli-seksultilit, tahalu-tehp mahtoqehsuwok eli-siktehpawolokuhtit posuwol. Tuciw Koluskap memhuwelomit, ipocol wolomahtu naka 'kotomakelkeskin. 'Tonheltomuwa. Miya-te peciyat, pomawsuwinuwok memhuwi-ktomakeyultiniya, nit milan kehceyawik wiyuhs. Nit msahkeyuwakon wikuwamihkuk, nit-te etoli-ksihkahsik.

When Koluskap appears, he see how frightened they are, like hares scared by a bobcat. Then Koluskap lets out a big laugh, for he is good-natured and merciful. He forgives them. It so happens at the time of his arrival that the people are extremely poor, so he gives them a lot of meat. Then the sorrow in the wikuwams all disappears.

Pukcinsqehs

Tree Stump Woman

Nit etoluteniyahtit skicinuwok—msi yaq-ote pokomkiyik. Peskuhs yaq wolomahtu naka 'piyemikinapiyin. Macehe ehtahsikiskahkil, nimiyanol 'tahtapiyil naka 'pahqiyil, 'tomhikon naka mihqotanis. Nehpaha musu naka muwiniyi, 'kotomakelkekhan msi-te. 'Kissoma ketomakeyilicihi. Tan etuci-apaciyalit, 'taskuhyaniya. 'Toqecimulaniya tan ehtek nehpahtaq. Tan etuci kisi-yahat, nit-tehc maciyapasiniya. Apatapasihtit, utapakonuwal etutonahsultihtit-otehc wiyuhs. Wot Pokomk sakom—Koluskap not—mihtaqsol muwiniyil.

There is a village of people—all, they say, are fishers. One of them in particular is very good-natured and braver that the rest. He goes out every day, taking along with him his bow and his arrows, his ax and his knife. He kills moose and bears, using all he kills for acts of kindness. He feeds the poor. When he returns, they are waiting for him. They ask him where his kill is. When he has told them, they set right out. When they return, their toboggans are all heavily loaded with meat. This fisher, Pokomk, is the chief—Koluskap—whose father is a bear.

Pukcinsqehs motewolon Pokomkesq. Ehpit, kisi kenoq skitapewehlosu tan-ote welitahatok. Yuhtol pemkiskahkil, skitapewiw yaq. Etuci-mocikit, musqitahamal sakomal. Pihce 'totoli-tpitahatomon tan-oc-olu 'toli-kisi-semahlan naka nekom wihqehtuwan 'tolitposuwakon.

Pukcinsqehs the motewolon is a she-fisher. Although she is a woman, she can change herself into a man whenever she pleases. These days, they say, she is a man. She is very evil, and she hates the chief. For a long time she has been thinking how she can remove him and take away his power.

Neqt pemkiskahk keti-maciyuthotihtit, Pukcinsqehs 'tiyal sakomal, "Pol wiciyemin, knaci-monawonapon."

One day, as they are getting ready to move, Pukcinsqehs says to the chief, "Come with me first, we'll go gather eggs."

Milawiyaniya oqitonuk, waht-ote pihcetu. Malom-ote peciyyik monihkuk, nit etoloqassihtit. Qeni-alonawonat Pokomk, Pukcinsqehs tuciw nekothat. Mace-sukin oqitonuk. Macentun, "Nokotha Pokomk monihkuk, nit-oc nil nsakomawin."

They go out in a canoe, far, far, away. At last they come to an island, where they land. Pokomk gathers eggs. Whereupon Pukcinsqehs leaves him. She paddles away in the canoe. She begins singing, "I have left Pokomk on the island, and now I shall be chief."

Nit 'peciyan utenehsisk. Wespasahkiwik msi-te maceyyik kcihkuk. Muck-ote pesq ma 'tasqessiwon. Welaqiwik wikkosiniya. Ehtahsikiskahkil 'taskuhyawal 'sakomamuwal. Malom-ote peciyak Pukcinsqehs sakomawiw— eli-pawatokopon-ote.

She arrives at the little village. In the morning, everyone leaves for the woods. Not even one is left behind. At night they make camp. Every day they wait for their chief. After a while Pukcinsqehs becomes chief—exactly what she has always wanted.

'Sanku kehsukonohok, sakom mihqitahamal witapiyil Qaqsossol motewolonuwiwol, kosona-al piluwapiyiw. Tuciw elintaq. Qaqsoss nutuwal, apeq pihcetu. Nit-te motapahan, macehomon monihkuk. Nit etoli-mskuwat sakomal.

On the thirteenth day, the chief remembers his friend Qaqsoss, the fox, who is a motewolon or possesses certain other powers. Thereupon he sings. Qaqsoss hears him, although it is far. Right away he goes down and starts swimming toward the island. There he finds the chief.

Neke tuciw Pokomk kotama kisi-pihcehomu. Qaqoss-olu 'tiyal elihc qsokahulat. Milawasukaniya. Qaqsoss 'tiyal, "Piskiqew naka kolahqaluwenin. Musa seksihkoc: nokosayiwc kmottokhomupon."

At that time, Pokomk could not swim far. But Qaqsoss tells him that he will ferry him across. They wade out into the water. Qaqsoss says, "Close your eyes and hang onto my tail. Don't be afraid: it will not be long before we reach land."

Nit-te-na mace-sewepehlan witapiyil. Mace-siktehsonit sakom, on kekeskossis 'tapskapin. Nomihtun wisoki-sopayiw iyuwok. Kotama wolamsotasiw. Litahasu, "Kotama kmottokassiw." Etolewestaq: "Kotama-tehc kmottokhomuhpon."

Then he begins to tow his friend. When the chief begins to tire, he opens his eyes just a little. He sees that they are very near the shore. He doesn't believe his eyes. He thinks, you will not get across. He speaks: "We will not reach land."

Qaqsoss 'tiyal, "Musa wolamsotasihkoc." Kenoq-olu 'pihcetahatomon.

Qaqsoss tells him, "Don't believe what you are thinking." He, however, thinks that there is still a long way to go.

Pokomk litahasu wahkehson elomelkimok, kenoq-olu tekkapimok-ote wisokolamson. 'Samaqan ansa wapinaqot. Pukcinsqehs 'kisehtun mocokiskot. 'Keki-te pomhomuk. Mesq piskiyanuhk, mottokhomoniya.

Pokomk thinks that there are but a few steps left. But as far as the eye can see it is very windy. The water really looks white. Pukcinsqehs has made it storm. All day they swim along. Before dark, they strike land.

"Nitap," itom Qaqsoss, 'tokec kisi-macaha."

"My friend," says Qaqsoss, "Now you can go on."

'Toliyan pokomkewi-wikuwamihkuk. Peciyat wikihtitpon, tehpu meskok sqotewamq. Naka cel kis tkiye.
Nit eli-nomihtaq 'kihkahan, on saku mace-nuhsuhkuwan.

He goes to the fishers' wikuwams. When he comes to where they had been living, he finds only the ashes of their fires, and they are already cold. Seeing that all have left, he starts to follow them.

'Keki-te wecuwawkuwa. Amsqahs tetomihkuwacil wikuwossol, 'pomiphal 'pahkamok Nimaqsuwehsuwol—Pokomk uhsimisol. Wikuwossol nihkaniw lapu, yat-olu Nimaqsuwehs apolapu.

All day he is getting closer to them. The first one he overtakes is his mother, who is carrying Nimaqsuwehs, the sable—Pokomk's younger brother—on her back. His mother is facing forward, but Nimaqsuwehs is looking back.

Pokomk eli-muskessit mipisishkuk, Nimaqsuwehs nomiyal. 'Titomon, "Weckuhyat nhesis."

When Pokomk appears from among the little bushes, Nimaqsuwehs sees him. He says, "Here comes my older brother."

Eli-qolopessilit wikuwossol, kotama-te wenil nomiyawiyil. Pokomk kisi-akuwessuss oposik. Nit-te mec-ote 'tolomuhsaniya.

When his mother turns, she sees no one. Pokomk has hidden behind a tree. So they keep on walking.

Apc Nimaqsuwehs 'kakaluwan, "Cu-tehlu nika, nomiya nhesis!"

Again, Nimaqsuwehs shouts, "Yes, really, mother, I do see my older brother!"

Apc wikuwossol qelopapessilit, 'keskuwapoman naka cel wolasuwewi-siktelomultiniya. Yat-olu Nimaqsuwehs, nit-te wetahkemok mipisisihkuk tahalu-tehp opos.

When his mother looks back again, she catches sight of him and they all smile affectionately at one another. Right away, Nimaqsuwehs gets dropped into the leaves as if he were a stick.

Pokomk 'tolokiman Nimaqsuwehsuwol, "Oliqasq wikuwamihkuk. Tan etuci-peciyayin, ktolihtun kci-sqot—wolokasqi-sqot—naka kossiyahkewan Pukcinsqehs nicanol. Naka kuckuwiphuwamin tan-ote kisi-tuciyayin."

Pokomk instructs Nimaqsuwehs, "Run to the village. When you arrive, build a big fire—a bark fire—and throw Pukcinsqehs's child into it. And then run to me as fast as you can move."

Elokimut, nit-te elluhket. Kisopotek sqot, 'kossiyahkan wasisol. 'Siktiyaqosan. Pukcinsqehs komac wisokiluwehe. Nit-te etuci-macephoqalat, tahalu-tehp malsom pemi-nuhsuhkuwat mahtoqehsuwol.

He does as he is instructed. When the fire is hot, he tosses the child in. He burns it to death. Pukcinsqehs is very angry. She chases after him as a wolf would pursue a hare.

Nimaqsuwehs komac wisokihpayu. Ahaciw ’tolomi-cipoki-kakaluwan, “Nhesis! Nsiwehs!”

Nimaqsuwehs is terrified. Louder and louder he calls, “My older brother! My brother!”

Pukcinsqehs-ona cipokihtaqsu, “Ktahcuwi-peciphus monihkuk eyit Pokomk wecihc kisaposiyusiyin.” Nit itomulit, nit-te-na Pokomk ’tehsaqotokkuwaman. Nemiyat Pukcinsqehs, nit-te ’seksin. Nit-te ’cipoki-siktelomin. ’Titomon, “Tehpu npahpuwi-nuhsuhkuwa, ipocol nmuhsacin Nimaqsuwehs.”

Pukcinsqehs shouts loud, too. “You’ll have to take yourself to the island where Pokomk is if you want to save yourself.” Just as she says this, Pokomk jumps on her. When Pukcinsqehs sees him, she is immediately afraid. Right away she laughs aloud. She says, “I was only chasing him in jest, for I am fond of Nimaqsuwehs.”

Kenoq-olu Pokomk wewitahamal. ’Tiyan, “Kociciyul, naka nkocichtun eleyyin, kil komac mocahant.”

Pokomk, however, knows what she is like. He says, “I know you and I know how you act, you terrible devil.”

Eli-piluwapiyit ’peciyamkun, ’tuwehkan ’tolsonuwakon. Nit etuci-sitahqehlat Pukcinsqehsuwol oposik, nit etoli-sici-nickisit. Kotama-te kisi-macehew. On macehkawotiniya Nimaqsuwehs naka Pokomk wikuwamok. Wot-olu Pukcinsqehs ponapsqi-tomhikonossis ’tihiness naka ’tolakonis. Komac sikoluhke eqeci-kisi-kettuhusit. Pokomk nutuwal metehtihikelicil ’qoci-tpuhk.

His power comes upon him, he uses his strength. He backs Pukcinsqehs up against a tree, and then she heals onto it. She can’t go anywhere. And Nimaqsuwehs and Pokomk start walking to the wikuwam. However, Pukcinsqehs had with her a stone ax and her wedge. She worked very hard to chisel herself loose. Pokomk heard her chopping away all night.

Wespasahkiwik Pukcinsqehs 'peciyan wikuwamihkuk. Kinhantuwinaqot opos kelomik 'pahkamok. Komac wihqinuwawal. 'Tolintuwamaniya, "Wot etoli-nokothat sakomal monihkuk, on toke 'kolihqahan sakom siciw oposik."

In the morning, Pukcinsqehs arrives at the wikuwams. A huge, ugly tree-stump is attached to her back. They think she is very funny-looking. They sing to her, "This is the one who left the chief on an island; now the chief sticks her onto a tree."

Nit Pukcinsqehs etuci-tqesiluwahat. 'Taskomi-macephuwaman skitapihi. Eli-yaliphuwet tahalu-te wiwonasi-malsom. 'Toloqiphuwan Pesamkuk. 'Topin kuwahsonuk. 'Titomon, "Tokec-olu keqsey-oc ntoli-kisi-qolopehlos wecihc kisi-wsikiyuk pomawsuwin?" Nit mehtewestaq, 'titomon, "Ncossuwewiyan!"

Then Pukcinsqehs is angry with shame. She runs away from mankind forever. She runs as a wild wolf would. She heads in the direction of Mt. Desert Island. She sits on an old log. She says, "Now how can I change myself so that I can torment mankind?" as she finishes speaking, she says, "I'll become a mosquito!"

Mec-ote toke pemkiskahk, tan toqiw eyihtit pokomk naka nimaqsuwehs, cossu 'tihin.

Even today, where both the fisher and the sable are found, so, too, is the mosquito.

Itasu, Pukcinsqehs-ona nekom nican utona kiwahqihkuk. Nican msiw mocinaqsultu. Kotokihi wasis macekona. 'Kisi-komutonatomuwan kotokihi ehpilicihi welikossultilicihi nicanuwa. Macekonan tahalu-te nekom nican, weci skat tqesihq etuci-ksikultilit nekom nican.

It is said that Pukcinsqehs gets her children by giants. All her offspring are hideous. She also raises other children. She raises them as her own offspring, so she will not be embarrassed that her own children are so ugly.

Neqt 'kisi-komutonalan skinuhsisol. Solahkiw 'tiyan. "Kat not kil kikuwoss."

Once she stole a boy. Suddenly, someone says to him, "That is not your mother."

Nemiyat 'pehenomum naka 'siwehs, ksikultuwok tahalu-te moci-weyossisok. Nit-ona elomahtuhtihtit. Nekom-olu woliku. 'Toqecimulan wikuwossol, "Keq nit weci-leyik?"

When he see his sisters and his brothers, they are very ugly, like evil animals. And that's the way they behave. But he is handsome. He asks his mother, "Why is this so?"

Wikuwossol 'toli-asitemkul, "Nikt kahk nomihqosultuponik nipayiw. Kil spotewi-wasis."

His mother answers him, "They were born at night. You are a child of the day."

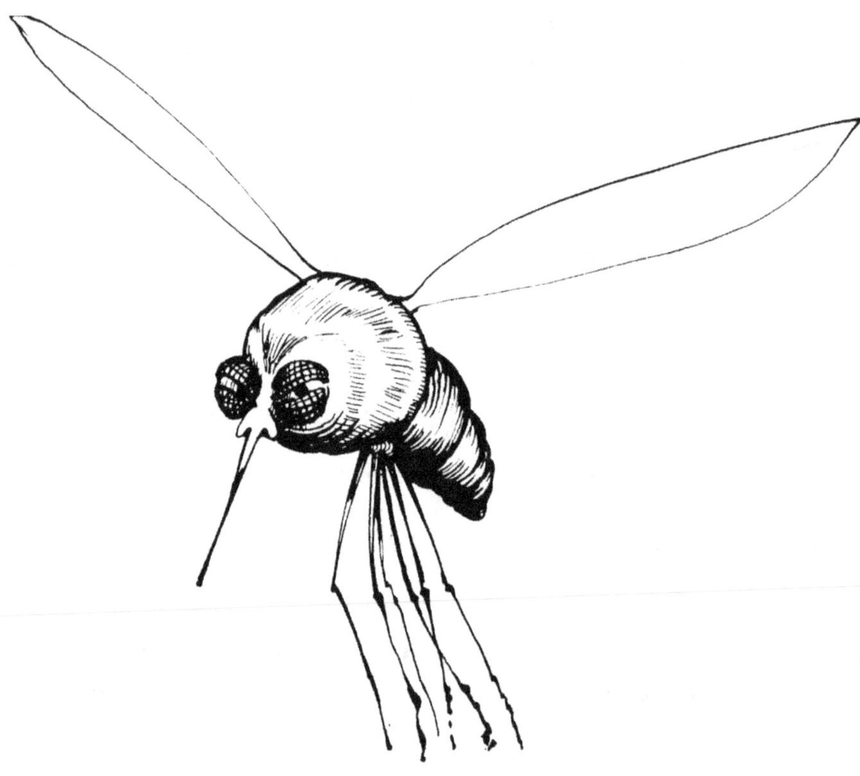

Kiwahqiyik

The Giants

Sakotiyamkiyak, nit wikit skitap, nisu 'qoss naka 'tusol. Msi-te kci-motewolonuwok. Msi-te-na kiwahqiyik. Mahawa pomawsuwinu—skitapihi, ehpilicihi, naka wasis. Msi-te keq 'tollukhotiniya ewapolikok, moci-luhkewakon. Skitkomiq, msi-te wenihi 'siwaciyawa, etuci-mili-wapololukhotihtit.

At Saco there lives a man, his two sons and his daughter. They are all great motewolons. Also, they are all giants. They devour people—men, women, and children. They do everything that is wrong—wicked deeds. On earth they have made everyone tire because of their many evil acts.

Neqt ewasisuwultilit, Koluskap witapehkamasoponihi. Mihtaqsuwal nekom-ona mihtaqsuwakumal, wesiwestilicihi nekom-ona 'siwehsuwakuma, 'pehenomumuwal nekom-ona 'pehenomumuwakumal. Pemikotonhotihtit nekom 'pomi-nutomon 'tuwapololuhkewakonuwa.

Once, when they were children, Koluskap had befriended them. He considered their father his father, the brothers his brothers, their sister his sister. As they grow older, he hears of their wicked deeds.

Koluskap 'titomon, "Nit ntoliyan, nqiluwahtun wolamewakon. Nit-olu wolamuhut, cuwihc mehciniyik. Kotama-tehc muck pesq sqittahawon tan wot pomawsuwinuwihpit. Kat-te keq leyiw tan tehpu wen."

Koluskap says, "I will go there and search for the truth. If they are proven wrong, they must die. Not even one shall be spared who devours people. It doesn't matter who it is."
This old man, the father of the motewolons and

Wot ktaqhomuhs, mihtaqsuwal motewolonuwok naka mihtaqsikacil toqiw, 'qotalokiqe naka epahsi-wapqe. Nit-ona Koluskap elehlosit. Nikt nisicik, kotama wewinuwawiyik wen not miyaw. Kessahat wikuwamok, 'sici-wolopessin ktaqhomuhsol.

his adopted father too, is one-eyed and half grey-haired. Koluskap assumes that same appearance. The two of them cannot be distinguished, one from the other. When he enters the house, he seats himself right next to the old man.

Nikt wesiwesticik nehpahtikewinuwok nutuwawal wenil metiyewestulicil. Kikimiw 'tuwapiniya, nomiyaniya pili-peciyalicil, 'tolinuwawal ansa mihtaqsuwal, kotama wewinuwawiwal wen wot miyaw. 'Titomoniya, "Kci-motewolon wot, kenoq-olu cuwi-qecehla, kosona macehe."

The two brothers, the murderers, hear someone speaking. Quietly they peek in, they see the newcomer; they think he looks like their father, they cannot tell which is which. They say, "This is a great motewolon, but he must be tested, or he will have to leave.

'Pehenomumuwal wihqehtun putepewi-soqon. 'Tolaqosomuwan kehci-wewisilicil. 'Punomon masqek pili-kisi-pqonhasik. Pesq wesiwesticik 'kossahan, wihqehtuwan. 'Tiyal, "Yut kahk kil 'sami-koluwot kmicin." Maceptun wikok.

Their sister takes a whale's tail. She cooks it for the great seeker of truth. She places it on freshly peeled birch bark. One of the brothers comes in and takes it away from him. He tells him, "This is too good for you to eat." He takes it to his house.

Koluskap 'titomon, "Tan yut milimok nit nil. Nit-tehc-ona weci-apaci-wihqehtu."

Koluskap says, "What is given to me is mine. That is why I am taking it back."

Tehpu sankewopu, 'tolitahatomon wesuwessic. Apacituwiyewiw, pokosson eyikpon ewecitu.

Sitting quietly, he wills it to come back. Back it comes flying, and lands where it was before.

'Titomoniya, "Wot kahk kci-motewolon, kenoq-olu cuwi-qecehla, kosona macehe.

They say, "This one is a great motewolon, but he must be tested, or he will have to leave."

Kisihpilit, 'peciptuwaniya kci-skonis, putepewi-tapehkikon. Kehci-skicinuwit 'toqeci-tomahkan. Etutsonit toqi-te 'pihtinol, tehpu kekesk 'tolakehtun. Milan Koluskapiyil. Ansa 'toli-tomahkan, tehpu 'cihcinol ewehkecil, tahalu-tehp 'tomakonahtoq.

When he has eaten, they bring him a great bone, a whale's jaw. The old man tries to break it. With the strength of both hands, he can only bend it a little. He gives it to Koluskap. He breaks it with such ease, using only his thumbs, as if it were a pipe stem.

Apc wesiwesticik itomuk, "Komac wot kci-motewolon, kenoq-olu cuwihc qecehla."

Again, the brothers say, "This is a very great motewolon, but he will have to be tested."

Nit 'peciptuwaniya kci-'tomakonol, eli-psonopit melihkikonewik 'tomawey: kotama tan tehpu eleyit skitap, skat motewolonuwihq, 'kisi-wtomektuwon. Nit wiwnonan, msi-te wen 'tome. Wesiwesticik 'tosalawal. Koluskap-olu, 'possonehlal. Neqt-ote wiqsonepal, msi-te 'kihkayaqote-te 'tomaweyaw.

Then they bring him a large pipe, filled with strong tobacco—no ordinary man, if he is not a motewolon, is able to smoke it. It is passed around, everyone smokes. The brothers inhale it. But Koluskap, he fills it. With one huge puff, all the tobacco is burned away.

'Titomoniya, "Komac wot kci-motewolon, kenoq-olu mec-otehc qecehla."

They say, "This is a very great motewolon, but still he will be tested further."

Mec-ote 'koti-mawi-wtomamaniya. Wikuwam wehqa-pskelute, litahatomuk 'patosikhaniya. Pesqon-ote eli-pkotesawet Koluskap tahalu-tehp tama tehsaqopit wocuk. Nekomaw-olu kotama aqamok 'kisi-kapuwihtmuwoniya. Itomuk, "Yut kahk kotama tepoluhkewakoniw. Naci-epeskomhotine."

They still want to smoke with him. Koluskap keeps smoking as if he were sitting somewhere on top of a mountain. They, however, can no longer bear it. They say, "This is not enough of a task. Let's go play ball."

Naci-epeskomhotihtit, Koluskap 'toli-nomihtun eli-toli-epeskomektuhtit cipinaqahk wosokiyatop, pemawsuwik. Cel mec tolapitehtehson qihiw woqonek. Wen-op apc wen piluwey skitap, cu-op 'tomotomakun 'sit. Kenoq-olu not Koluskap piluwapiyiw.

When they go to play ball, Koluskap sees that they are using for the ball a horrible-looking skull, which is still alive. It is still even snapping its teeth near his heel. If this were any other man, it would surely bite off his foot. But Koluskap is one of extraordinary powers.

Etuci-siktelomit. 'Titomon, "Nit kahk koti-layyawolotiyeq, wolikon. Kenoq-olu yat-tehc wen 'tuwehkahal 'tepeskomakonumol."

He starts laughing. He says, "If that is how you want to play, good. But each one will use his own ball."

Tuciw epeskomehlukosit oloqiw sopayiw sipuk. ’Tomahkan psketqon. ’Qolopihtehmon wosokiyatop aqami-cipinaqahk katok kotok. Motewolonuwok macephuwolotuwok, tahalu-tehp apiqosikon macehpawolat mahtoqehsu. Ansa-te woli-piyemhantuwikotuwak.

So, he plays the ball over toward a tree by the edge of the river. He breaks off a knot. He turns it into a skull more horrible-looking than the other. The motewolons flee, like hares frightened away by a lynx. They are really outdone.

Nit Koluskap 'tomanokihtehkmon ktahkomiq. Pitpewiyak 'samaqan sakhessik, weci-pecicuwok pemotonihkek. Msi-te ktahkomiq kintaqot. Tuciw Koluskap elintaq. 'Tolintuwakon ewehket, msi-te 'kisi-qolopehla. Nikt wesiwesticik naka mihtaqsuwal nomehswiyawolotuwok, maciyehlukultiniya eli-pitpek 'samaqan (skitapiyik al-ote olkilultuwok), malom-ote supekuk etolitomek. Nit-tehc etoleyawultihtit askomiw.

Then Koluskap stamps a hole through the surface of the earth. Foaming water appears, flowing down from the higher ground. All the earth resounds loudly. At that instant, Koluskap starts to sing. With his song, he transforms them all. Those brothers and their father turn into fish; they float away in the foaming water—they are about as big as men—and eventually to the deep salt water. That will be their home forever.

Espons
Raccoon

Neqt welokiskahk spasahkiw, Laks macewsan, esponsuwehlosu. Qeni-yaliyat skitkomiq mecimiw, kisi-mili-acehlosu. Nit pemuhset, solahkiw nihkaniw weckuhyat kci-muwin. Komac wolitahasu nemiyat esponsol. Nit-te muwin 'kisitahatomon nehpahan, tehpu oli-kisehtaq. Pol 'koti-wsikiyal eli-milomahtulit... naka komac 'kotuhpin.

One fine morning, Laks starts walking, having assumed the shape of a raccoon. When he used to roam the earth, he could at that time change himself into whatever form he desired. As he is walking, all of a sudden coming in front of him is a big bear, Muwin. He is very happy to see Espons, the raccoon. Right then and there Muwin decides to kill him, if only he can manage it. First he will punish him for the many ways he has behaved—and besides, he is very hungry.

Espons-olu nit-te macephuwan, 'pistehsinon piqekit opos. Muwin mace-keccopskahan. Espons 'kocicihtun elihc opos kipiyat, nit-tehc-ona nekom macahan. Espons 'posqentun tahalu-tehp skat wetomitahamahq muwiniyil: "Tan-otehc kehsalkiyin naka tan kehsi-ksomonot wot opos, kat-tehc kmosoniw. Sehta-pisessiyin weciyay, on yakahc kmosonin, nit-tehc nmehcinan. Nit kat-tehc ktoli-kisehtuwon tan qeni-apsalokosit opos."

But Espons immediately starts running away, and he dives into a hollow tree. Muwin starts uprooting it. Espons knows that the tree will fall, and then he will get away. Espons bursts into song as if he were not worried about Muwin at all. "However much you dig and however much you push on this tree, you will not catch me. If you back in where I came in, then you will get me and I will die. But that you cannot do while the hole in the tree is small."

Muwin nutuwat, wolamsotuwal. Kenoq-olu nomihtun nit nokomasi-kisi nekom kinalokehtun. Weckuwi-pisessilit, espons 'pokkikalan; 'totoli-sakolonan tokkiw mehcinelit. Nit espons nutiyapekin,'toliyan molocessis muwinewiyeya. Apc-ote mec macewsan.

When Muwin hears him, he believes him. However, he sees that he can easily enlarge the hole. When he makes his way in, Espons grabs him; he grips him tightly until he is dead. Then Espons crawls out; he makes little bearskin mittens. And then he resumes his walk.

Kesq yut pemuhset, solahkiw ehtek wikuwam, sakhi-pkotetek. ’Kossahan, neqtelakutulticik pokomkehsisok lamikuwam. Ulima. ’Tiyan, “Wasistuk, nasqihiq, ktapenkuloniyakc yukt muwinewiyeyak nmolocessok.”

While he is walking along, suddenly there in front of him is a wikuwam, with smoke rising out of the top. He enters; there, inside, is a family of baby fishers. He talks to them pleasantly. He says to them, “Children, comb me. I will pay you with these bearskin mittens of mine.”

Nit pokomkehsisok nasqahaniya; 'possetokahmuwaniya naka 'putuwatomuwaniya 'soqon. Nit-te etoli-kposki-nasqahahtit. Etuci-kotuhpultihtit pokomkehsisok, on mahaniya espons molocess. Kisi-pqonaskihputuhtit wiyuhs, natahqosiniya naka mahaniya. Espons tuhkiyat, 'kinapoma naka naskahtaqsuwaman. 'Tiyan, "Tan nil muwinewiyeyak nmolocessokk?"

Then the little fishers comb him; they part his hair and they blow on his tail. They keep grooming him and he falls asleep. The little fishers are so hungry that they eat Espons's mittens. Scraping off the meat, they cook them and eat them. When Espons wakes up, he stares sharply at them and speaks to them angrily. "Where are my bearskin mittens?" he says.

Siktehpayultuwok. 'Toli-asitemawal. "Nkisaqosannuk naka nmahanen."

They are frightened. "We cooked them and ate them," they reply.

Nit-te espons 'qiltuwan. Nokosanaqot nokka-koskotunenan. Tehpu motehsanol putomacil: mesq-ona 'tawew. Espons litahasu kat-tehc kisacomiw.

Then Espons goes after them. In no time at all, he strangles every one. The youngest is the only one he does not get, but he does not know how to talk anyway. Espons thinks he won't be able to tell what happened.

Nit Espons wihqehlan mehcinelicihi pokomkehsis naka 'sehkewolan elkepolasik weci-sakhiyat kci-pokomk, naka moqtuniyaqhan. Weci-litahasit, "Weckuwi-wolitahasulticik nicansisok." Nit wiwisahtehkuwan. " Etuci-wolitahasossultihtit nemiyihtit." Peciyat, kotama-te-olu wen macessiw. Nit 'piluwitahasin, keqoss wapolessu. Komac nokosa-qolopitahasu, msahkeyu. Solahki-te motehsan nutuwal wikuwossol. 'sakhotqihin elomalokahsok. Mec 'sami-wasisuwiw 'kisacomin, kenoq-olu komac 'sotuweyu. 'Pokkikatomon mokoses, 'totoluwikhusin eli-kecalokiqat naka wiwoniw 'tunok.

Then Espons picks up the little dead fishers, and propping their mouths open, stands them up on the path where the big fisher will come out. Then she will think, "My little children are coming so happily." She hurries towards them. "How happy the little ones are to see me." When she gets near them, none of them moves. Then she becomes suspicious, something is wrong. Very quickly her thoughts change, she is grief-stricken. All of a sudden the littlest fisher hears his mother. He jumps out from a little hole. He is still too young to be able to tell what happened, but he is very clever. Grabbing a piece of charcoal, he marks himself around the eyes and around his mouth.

"Aha!" mihtaqsol itomul, "not kahk nkociciya. Espons not!" Nit-te-na macephoqalan. Nanakiw tetomihkuwat pokomk, wisokiluwehenaqsu. Wiwonapekehtun oposiyahqem tahaluhp skitap. Espons 'tolapoman. "A ... kotama kahk oposiyahqem nkisi-nehpuhukuwon. Pkuwahqiyasq yaka nehpihit-oc."

Pokomk-ona 'kocicihtun eliyat: 'toliyan elomi-walcokek, 'peciptun pesqonul, nit tekomat Esponsol tan-al etutahket. Nit pasktehson, sipelihtuwehtehson Espons woniyakonok naka kolomessu eli-puspek. Tepot-olu 'tolitahasin Pokomk, "Espons nit wilitpan msi-te nutehtehmuwan." On yaka macahan.

Nit Espons etoli-sankewossit tokkiw Pokomk macahat, nekom-ona macahan. Kci-motewolon kahk nakaw, kenoq wahkehsossu weleyuwacihi.

Nit elomiyat, 'pecuhsan eyultihtit kceyawiwok ehpicik etolikonahticihi wasis. 'Tiyan, "Komac menakaceyu eli-macekoneq wasisok. Nilun nokosakonannuk."

Nikt woli-ehpicik 'tiyaniya, "Tan-op-olu apc tan ntoli-kisikonanen?"

"Nit-te knostuhmuloniya nilun ellukhotiyek. Pawatomek nokosakiniya, nkihcitapeqithannuk 'samaqanok 'qoci-tpuhk. Ipa pesq mahkuwiyiq. Knostumuloniyahc ellukhotiyeq koti-nokosakoneq."
Milaniya peskuwol. Macephan sipuk.

"Aha!" says his father, Pokomk, the fisher, "I know that one. That's Espons!" Immediately he starts chasing after him. Soon Pokomk overtakes him, looking very angry. He swings a club as a man would. Espons looks at him. "Ah... a club cannot kill me. A cattail is what will kill me."

Pokomk knows just where to go for them: he goes down towards the swamp, gathers a few, then strikes Espons as hard as he possibly can. They splatter on impact, flow down over Espons's head and stick where it is wet. But Pokomk thinks, "That is Espons's brain that I have splattered." Only then does he leave.

Espons lies there very still until Pokomk is gone, then he also leaves. He was a great motewolon, that one, but there were very few he treated kindly.

As he goes further, he comes to a place where many women are nursing children. He tells them, "How very slowly you raise your children. We raise them fast."

Those good women say to him, "Well, how then are we to raise them?"

"Well, I will tell you what we do. When we want them to grow fast, we soak them in the water all night. Here, let me have one. I'll show you what to do if you want to raise them quickly."

'Ketoloqtahan pqomiyil naka 'pisehlan wasisol. Wespasahkiwik naciphan. Muskehlat, assokitahasultuwok-ote ehpicik eli-assoki-kisehtulit. Nit msi-te kehsihtit ehpicik 'punaniya nicansisuwa sipuk apc welaqiwik. Nit-te-na Espons uci-wiwisa-macahan. Wasisok-olu msi-te wapalokiqewocossultukk. Mehcinhotukk.

They give him one. He takes him to the river. He chops away the ice and puts the child in. In the morning he gets him. When he pulls him out, the women are surprised indeed at the wonder of his accomplishment. That night, every one of the women puts her child into the river. At that point, Espons hurriedly departs. But all the children's eyes have turned white with the cold. They are all dead.

Apc kotok wikuwam 'peciyan, etolelucik ehpicik. Wolikon ewehkehtit motekoninaqahk etolihtuhtit ptoqapiyil. 'Tiyan, "Komac menakacinaqot eli-lihtuweq yuhtol. Nilun nucikansonnuk naciqenomonennul sqotewamkuk. Coke miliq ewehkemok, ktokehkimoloniya."

Then he comes to another wikuwam, where there are many women. Using fine skins, they are making pouches. He says to them, "How very slowly you make these. In our homes, we roll them in ashes. Here, give me the material, I will teach you."

Milaniya pesqon. 'Punomon etoli-ksamkolek sqotewamkuk. Wahkehs eli-nehsemok muskamqehtun. Weluwikhasik naka wolikon toqap. Ahsitahasultuwok. Nit-te msiw wiciqenomoniya-na nekomaw. Muskehtuhtit, msi-te wihqihtahtetul naka 'kihkayaqotetukkol. Msi-te wekihtuniyal. On apc macahan.

They give him one. He puts it in the hottest glowing part of the ashes. After a few breaths, he pulls it from the coals. It is a well-made and beautifully designed pouch. Now they are tempted into doing it. So all of them roll theirs in the ashes too. When they take them out, every one of them is shriveled and burnt to a crisp. They have ruined them all. And again he goes on his way.

Mam-ote peciye kci-sipuk. Kat-te 'kocicihtuwon tan-oc 'toli-kisi-qsokassin. Yut elapit sipuwahkuk, nomiyan pemahqossinulit kci-wiwilomeqiyil, tahalu liku kci-akotalahq. 'Kapu. Espons 'tiyan, "Muhsumi, qsokahulin okamok."

Eventually he comes to a big river. He does know how he is to get across. Looking along the riverbank, he sees Wiwilomeq, a giant slug, stretched out—he looks like a big alligator. He is blind. Espons says to him, "Grandfather, take me across."

"Kehtol-al, nqenoss, tepess npahkamok." Nit-te-na macehomon. Kahkakuhsok naka yukt kci-kakakok mace-malikimaniya. "Keq nikt itomuk sipsisok?" 'toli-qecikesin wiwilomeq.

"Of course, my grandson, get onto my back." Then he starts swimming. At that point, the crows and the big ravens begin to laugh at him. "What are those birds saying?' asks Wiwilomeq.

"Itomuk, Wiwisay, wiwisaphan not espons kotuwaposiktuwon kpomawsuwakon." Nit wiwilomeq kotama nomihtuwon ktahkomiq. Kesq-ote eli-wisokiyat, mam-ote cocokahtehsin. Epahsiw-te peci-olonomtehsin sipuwahkuk. Espons 'kahpotatqihin. Wiwisa uci-'ci-macahan.

"They say hurry, go fast with that raccoon if you want to save your life." Wiwilomeq does not see the land in front of him. Hurrying along, he runs aground, he plunges halfway into the riverbank. Espons jumps off. He leaves from there in a great hurry.

Nit elomiyat, 'pecuhsan saqteminihkuk. 'Tiyan, "Tan-pal ktolkuwiniya nil muhuleq?"

Going along, he comes to a blackberry patch. He says to them. "How would you affect me if I were to eat you?"

"Kmockulponc Espons, ipocol nilun msiw psuliminok."

"We would affect you badly, Espons, because we are all choke-berries."

"Nita, kotama kpawalluhpa."

"Oh no, I don't want you."

Mec-ote elomiyat, moskuwa kikcokalokiqemins. "Tan-oc ktolkuwiniya muhuleq?"

Continuing on his way, he finds some rose hips. "How will you affect me if I eat you?"

"Kikcokkulpon ehtahc, nilun msiw kikcokalokiqeminsok."

"We will make you itch for sure; we are all itch-berries.

"A … nit-te miyaw nil eli-pawatom," oli-asitewtom. Mitsin. Mam-ote memihpu. Macahan. Solahki-te peci ma seski-miyawomolsiw, stehpal wesikiyiht keqseyal elonomik. On 'kikcokapehlosin. Kotama-te wicuhkemkuwon. Mam-ote moskomon kawapskek ponapsq, nit esuwacqessit tokkiw mehtwehpusit 'qocik. Mec-ote toke pemkiskahk wewinaqot eli kotama piyehsuwihq 'qocik espons.

"Ah… exactly what I want," he answers. He eats. At last he eats his fill. Off he goes. Suddenly he begins to feel very sick, as if something painful were piercing him. And he proceeds to scratch himself. It does not help him. At last he finds a rough rock; there he rubs back and forth until the hair comes off his rear end. Still, even today, it can be seen that the raccoon has no hair on his rear end.

Nit-te-na mehtapeksin.

And that's the end of him.

Cihkonaqc

Turtle

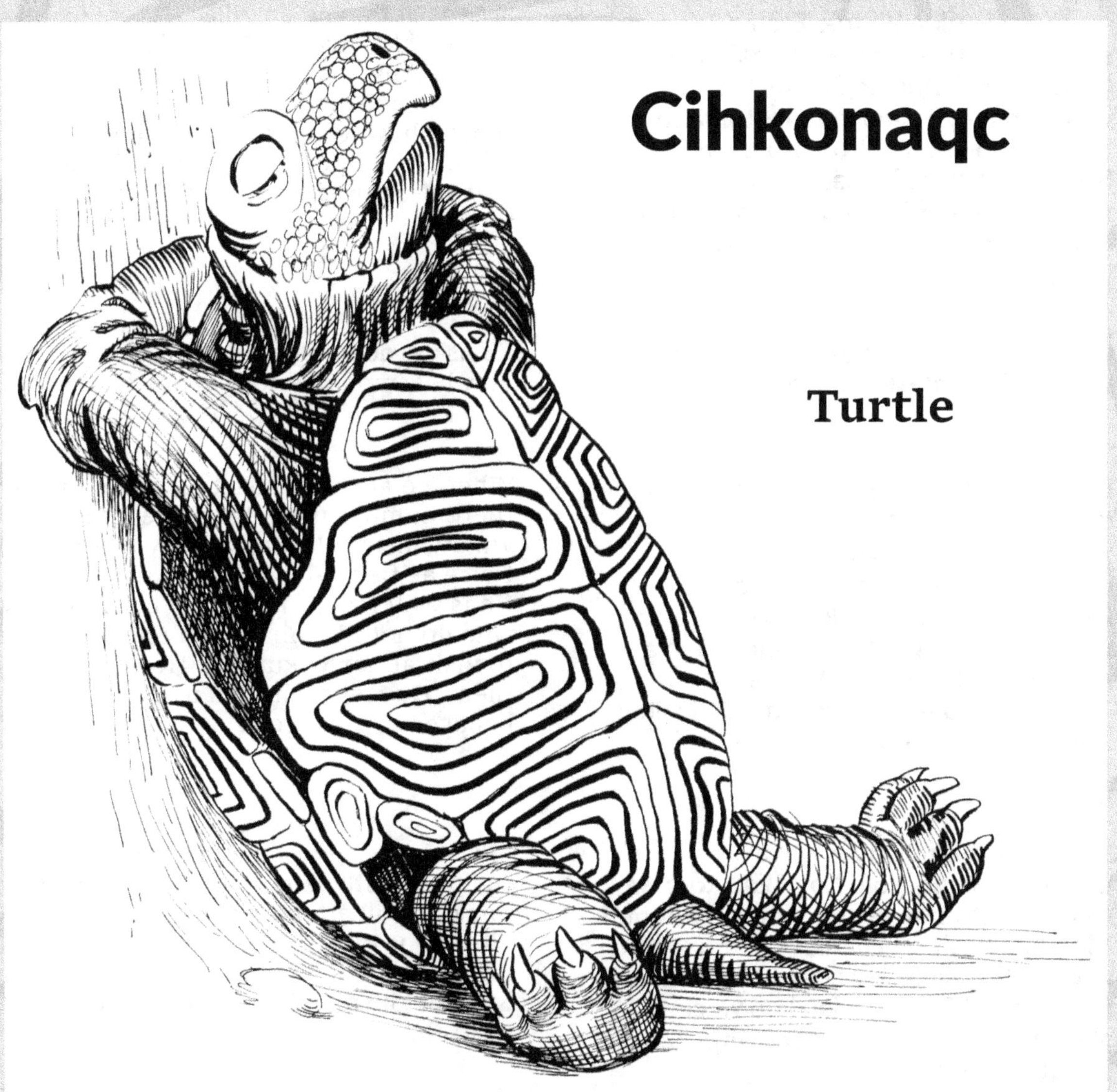

Koluskap weci-macahat Oktokomq, macewehket oqiton. 'Peci-sukin Piktuk. Etoli-peciyat skicinuwi-utenek, nit etoli-mskuwat nicalkul Cihkonaqcol. Komac Cihkonaqc wisoki-maleyu naka menakatomahtun. Itomuk, "Eluwehk-al-ote Koluskap nicalkul." Kenoq-olu kotokik litahasuwok nit-al nit Cihkonaqc 'kisikonuwakon. Kenoq etuci-wolomahtaq, nit Koluskap muhsaci-wihqehlal.

When Koluskap leaves Newfoundland, he goes by canoe. He paddles to Pictou. When he arrives at the Indian village, there he finds his uncle Cihkonaqc (Turtle). Cihkonaqc is very lazy, and his manner is extremely slow. They say, "He must indeed be Koluskap's uncle." Others, however, think that it is a result of Cihkonaqc's upbringing. Nevertheless, he is so good-natured that Koluskap has a fondness for him.

On Koluskap 'kisitahatomon 'qolopehlan weci-kisi-sakoli-skitapewilit.

Koluskap decides to transform him so that he may be a man of strong character.

Peciyat Piktuk, pemikhoticik aqamok 'qotatq wikuwamol. Koluskap wisoki-wolapewiw, nisokehs oli-seskapewiw katok-op sakom. Ksi-muhsalqosu. Wahkehsu ehpit skat muhsalahq. Msi-te 'pawatomuwaniya 'peciyalin yat-te wen wikuwak. 'Tosaha-na nomiyan. Nisininiyal nicalkul, assokomahtuwol.

When he arrives at Pictou, those living there number more than one hundred wikuwams. Koluskap is very handsome, twice as fierce-looking as a chief would be. He is well loved. There are but few women who do not like him. Each one desires him to visit at her wikuwam. He refuses to see them. He stays with his uncle, the one who behaves so strangely.

Koti-kceyawi-mawiyan naka pahpultin, kenoq-olu Koluskap kotama 'toloqitahatomuwon 'toliyan pahpultimok. Mec-ote-olu 'toqecimulal Cihkonaqcol witayyalin. 'Tiyal, "Msi-tehc 'tiyultiniya naksqiyik." 'Toqecimulan keq weci skat cpahkatomuhk. "Kat cuwitpotu knoqtuhkayin."

There is going to be a big gathering complete with games, but Koluskap does not think he will attend the festival. Still, he asks Cihkonaqc to participate. He tells him, "All the young girls will be there." He asks him why isn't he married. "You should not live by yourself."

"Etuci-ehta ktomakeyi, muck-ote kotama pesqonuwiw ntoloqtewakon tan yut welkomawik mawiyamok. Kamot-op nil ntotoli-wtoman nikok."

"I am so poor, I don't even have one bit of clothing good enough for the gathering. It is far better for me to sit at home and smoke."

"Nit kahk-ona tehpu oli-pawalqahk," Koluskap 'toli-asitemal nicalkul, "musa 'tomitahatomuhkoc. Tan kahk wen piluwitposit, nokomasitahatomon tahalu eli-acehtasik loqtewakonol."

"If that is all that is wanted," Koluskap answers his uncle, "don't worry. He who possesses unusual powers thinks it is an easy task to do something like changing clothing."

“Aha, ntuwasom,” itom Cihkonaqc. “Mec-op-al-op-olu kisi-acihtuwan ’tolamhok pomawsuwin?”

“Yes, my child,” says Cihkonaqc “but is it possible for you to change the inside of a person?”

“Nita,” eli-asitewtok sakom, “nit sikeyu ellukhotimok. Mesq nokotomuwan yut utenehsis, ntolluhkanc nit. Kil-otehc-ona yut toke ktoliyan elayyawolotimok; nahseht nkospisun.”

“Well, now,” answers the chief, “that is a difficult task. Before I leave this little village, I will do that. But now, you will attend the games; put on my belt.”

Nit-te kisi-nahsonok, Cihkonaqc ’peci-wisoki-wolapewin tan tehpu skitap kosona ehpit mesq ’toli-nomihtuwon. Koluskap nahsonomuwan peyemi-koluwahkil loqtewakonol. ’Toli-tpahmuwal tokkiw mehciyak ’kiskumol nekom-otehc peyemi-wolapewit skitap.

As soon as he has put it on, Cihkonaqc becomes so handsome no man or woman has ever seen the like before. Koluskap dresses him in the most valuable clothing. He promises him that to the end of his days he will be the most handsome of all men.

On Cihkonaqc ’toliyan etoli-mawiyamok.

And so Cihkonaqc goes to the gathering.

Wot-olu sakom Piktuk nuhu wisoki-woliku ’tus, pciliw ewasisuwit. Nihtol nemiyacil. Wesuwessin. ’Titomon, “Nomiya pawatom.” Yukt tokec msi-te skinuhsuwok Piktuk ’pawatomoniyal yuhtol naksqiyil. Nehpahawal tan wot mesonat.

Now the chief at Pictou has three very beautiful daughters, especially the youngest. That’s the one Cihkonaqc sees. He goes back. He says, “I’ve seen the one I want.” Now the youths at Pictou all want this girl. They’ll kill the one who wins her.

Nit etuci Koluskap wihqonok naka maceptun wapap, naci-kolulwewan Cihkonaqcol. Wewikuwossit, ulitahamal Cihkonaqcol. Nit-te-na naksq ’tolonekhan pileya stahqonu, ’sipelekehlan kci-wapsqewiyil. ’Toliyaman Cihkonaqcol, naka kespahtek wiyuhs ’toli-wolaqihpiniya. Nit toqi-te ’kisi-nisuwiniya.

Taking wampum, Koluskap goes to negotiate on behalf of Cihkonaqc. The mother, she accepts Cihkonaqc. and so the youngest girl arranges a bed of new boughs; she spreads out a big white bearskin. She goes to Cihkonaqc and they eat an evening meal of dried meat. So the couple is married.

Cihkonaqc wisoki-maleyu. Kotokik ketunkahtihtit, nekom kahk lossin wikok. Neqt pemkiskahk nisuwihticil ’tiyukun. “Nit-olu skat keq koti-olluhkewon, nokosayiwc ksiktelamipon.”

Cihkonaqc is extremely lazy. While others hunt, he just stays home, lying around. One day, his wife says to him, “If you don’t do something, we’re going to starve soon.”

Nit nahsonan 'takom. Ehpit nuhsuhkuwan naci-kotunkelit: 'koti-nomiyal tan 'tolluhkalin. Kotama pihcetu oliyew, on napisqaman, 'qastehsinon, cel ksihtehsimsu. Nisuwihticil nit-te wesuwessin, naci-yahan wikuwossol, "Cihkonaqc kat-te keq lawotiw."

So he puts on his snowshoes. The woman follows him as he goes hunting—she wants to see what he does. He does not go far before he trips and injures himself. Quickly his wife returns to her mother, "Cihkonaqc isn't worth a thing."

Wikuwossol-olu itom, "Temonuk keq olluhke. Cikihtuwan."

But her mother says, "Later he'll do something. Leave him alone."

Neqt pemkiskahk Koluskap 'tiyal Cihkonaqcol, "Sepawonuk koti-kci-mawi-epeskomhotin. Kil-ona ktahcuwi-toli-wiciyan. Ipocol msi-te knacitahamkuk skinuhsisok yut, ktoqecihc nehpuhukuk. Ktomokuhukukc naka ktomokipilkun. Etuci nit leyik, qihiw-oc kti ksilhuss wikok.

One day, Koluskap tells Cihkonaqc, "Tomorrow everyone is getting together for a big ball game. You also must participate. Since all the young men here hate you, they will try to kill you. They'll pile up on you and trample you. When that happens, you will be near your father-in-law's house.

"Kisihc qesimuhtuwak. Kmillonc piluwapiyuwakon wecihc kisi-pasittoqqiyin nisokehs; kenoq-olu nuhuwewey komac-oc mocessu, kenoq-olu cuwi-leyu."

"You will be able to escape them. I'll give you the power of supernatural illusion so that you'll be able to jump over the house twice; the third time, however, it will go very badly, but this must happen."

Msi-te-na leyu yuhutpon. Skinuhsisok 'toqeci-nehpahawal. Eli-qesimuhtuwat, cuwi-pasittokku wikuwamok tahalu-tehp toke sips qesicituwiyat, kenoq-olu nuhuwewey napittehsinon wikuwami-oposiyahqihkuk. Nit-te ekhucit, etoliluwahat pkotek. Wikpolahsu weci-pkotetek emehkew.

All that is told to him happens. The young men try to kill him. In escaping them he jumps over the wikuwam as a bird would swoop; but on the third time he is caught on the wikuwam poles. There he hangs, angrily, in the smoke. He is dried and hardened by the smoke rising from below.

Wot-olu Koluskap lamikuwam epits. 'Tiyan, "Nicaloq, koti-sakomawehlol, kci-sakom cihkonaqcok."

Now Koluskap was sitting inside. He says, "Uncle, I'm going to make you chief, the great chief of the turtles."

Etuci-wikpolahsat Cihkonaqcol. Mam-ote motekonum cikonaqstek. Eli-cilaqositpon mec-ote wewinaqot toke pemkiskahk. 'Kisi-na nuteloksehlan, pesqon tehpu cilkeyossik esqonasik.

He continues to cure Cihkonaqc with the smoke. At last his skin is shriveled and hard. How he was scorched can still be seen today. Also, he cuts out his intestines, leaving only one short one.

On Cihkonaqc 'cipoki-kakaluwan, "Keka knehpihi!"

And Cihkonaqc yells out loud, "You're almost killing me!"

Kenoq-olu Klouskap 'tasitemal, "Kotama leyiw. Kmillon kci-pomawsuwakon. Tokec-oc 'ci-maciw kisi-tehc yali-topskans etolamkolek, kisihc pomaws ktahkomikuk naka 'samaqanok. Cika-te tomiqehtuhukiyin, mec-otehc kpomaws esqonatek kehsukoniw. Peci-tehc kmoshun, tolihtehsonc kisi-monehtasik sipkiw."

But Koluskap replies, "That's not true. I am giving you great life. From now on you will be able to roll in the fire, you will be able to live on land and in the water. Even if your head is cut off, still you shall live for nine days. And even your heart will beat for a long time after it is taken out."

Komac Cihkonaqc wolitahasu yut peci-leyik. Msi-te elehlut 'kisuwehkan.

Cihkonaqc is very happy when this happens. All that has been done to him he can now use.

Wespasahkiwik msiw skitapiyik kotunkahtuwok. Koluskapiyil 'tahkinuwehtakul, "'Qiluwahtuniyahc tan ktoli-kisi-nehpuhukun."

In the morning, all the men go hunting. Koluskap informs him, "They are going to look for a way to kill you."

Skinuhsisok nihkanapasuwok, Cihkonaqc asit nakahkalsu. Kenoq-olu sesolahkiw motewolonuwituwiye. 'Qesqicituwiyan spiqiw woniyakonuwak. Kotama nomiyaw. Mulahkek pemahqihkek, nit etoli-nehpahat musuwol. 'Tolacqiman akomawtik. Ketunolihcihi petapasilit, tehsaqopu musok, etoli-wtomat, etolaskuwasit.

The young men walk ahead, Cihkonaqc hides himself behind. But all of a sudden, he makes a magic flight. He soars over their heads. He is not seen. Deep in the forest, there he kills a moose. He drags it to the snowshoe path. When his enemies come along, he is sitting on top of the moose, smoking, waiting.

Nit eli-peciyak, msi-te aqami-musqitahasultuwok. 'Kisolumaniya nehpahaniya Cihkonaqcol naka Koluskapiyil.

So it comes to pass that they hate him all the more. They decide to kill Cihkonaqc and Koluskap.

Keti-macahat Koluskap, on 'tiyukun tan-oc ellukhotihtit. "Amsqahs-otehc motutuwatomoniya kci-sqot. Nit-tehc kil kossiyahkalkun. Nicaloq, kulitahasuwi-oliyan: etutsonuwik ntolsonuwakon kotamahc kusikawsiw. Nit-tehc 'topolutomoniya kpiscopolokun. Nit kolamuwan: Musa nit leyic! Aqami-tehc 'toli-koti-ollukhotiniya. Kmikahkaman. Mec-otehc-olu leyu."

When Koluskap is going to leave, he tells Cihkonaqc what they will do. "First of all, they will build a great fire. And then they'll throw you in. Uncle, go happily; with my great powers you shall not suffer. Then they will talk about drowning you. At that, you stop them, saying, Don't let it happen! They will want to do it even more. Fight them. However, it will still happen."

Nit eli-itok, peciye. Cihkonaqc wolitahasu. 'Tatiyuhewikotuwan Koluskapiyil.

What he says comes to pass. Cihkonaqc is pleased. He says adieu to Koluskap.

On skinuhsisok 'pokkikalaniya Cihkonaqcol. 'Kossiyahkaniya sqotek. On 'qolopossinon naka 'kuwin: maleyu-na. Yut mehtamkolek sqot, 'tuhkiyan, apc wiqtehmon piwsokul, ipocol tki-tpuhkot.

And the youths grab Cihkonaqc. They throw him into the fire. And he rolls over and falls asleep—he is lazy, you know. When the fire burns out, he wakes up; he asks for more wood, for the night is cold.

Apc 'pokkikalaniya, nostuhmuwaniya 'piscopolaniya. Nit yaka sikte-nokatok. 'Tiyan, "Musa nit leyic! Kamot-op knukcoktihiniya katok kcuwahpahkaliniya."

Again they seize him; they tell him they are going to drown him. That he is terribly afraid of. He says, "Don't let it happen! Better you should cut me to pieces than throw me in the water."

Nit weci-kisolutomuhtit maciyacqimaniya. Nit 'cipokihtaqsin, ayut siki-mikahket. 'Keccopskehla oposiyi. Muskapskehtun ponapskul, ayut wocopskiyil, tahalu wen wenatominet. 'Tepehlaniya oqitonuk, macehulaniya epahsakom. Nit etoli-cuwahpahkehtit. 'Totolosakiyaniya tokkiw nekkomapomahtit elomi-ktapahalit.

That is why they decide to drag him away. Then he shouts and struggles very hard. He uproots trees. He tears up the rocks and the roots just like a crazy man. They load him into a canoe, and take him to the middle of the lake. There they throw him in. they watch him until they can no longer see him sinking.

Wespashkiwik wisokolate. Keq nomihtuniya etoli-macetutomuwik kci-ponapskuk tama-al tekkapimok. Nisuwok skinuhsuwok wihqnomoniya oqiton, milawi-sukiniya, natsakihtuniya keqsey nit. Nit-te peci-sukihtit, peciwehse. Kci-monossapskuk nemq-ote sakpetul, nit Cihkonaqc elossit, etoli-ksalosuhket.

In the morning, it is quite warm. They see something moving on a big rock near the horizon. Two youths take a canoe; they paddle out to see what it is. As they arrive in the canoe, the wind picks up. On some big rocks, barely sticking up out of the water, there lies Cihkonaqc, sunning himself.

Nomiya weckuhyalit, 'kocicihtun naci-wihqehloku. 'Tatiyuhewikotuwan, olomi-cuwahpi-tepoqonessuwa. Mec-ote toke msiw cihkonaqcok nemiyahtit wenil, nit-te 'cuwahpi-tepoqonessultiniya.

He sees them coming, and knows they are going to get him. He bids them adieu, disappearing into the water heels first. Even today, all turtles, when they see someone, disappear in the water heels first.

Cihkonaqc nomiyan nisuwihticil. Wolitahasuwi-pomawsuwok cel nicaniwok. Nit oli-peciye, elomi-kehsukoniwik, Koluskap naci-nomiyan nicalkul. Wasis sasotemu. "Knostuwa itok?" Koluskap metiyewestaq.

Cihkonaqc goes to see his wife. They live happily, and they have a child. It happens, after a time, that Koluskap goes to see his uncle. The child is crying. "Do you understand what he is saying?" Koluskap is heard to say.

"Kotama," Cihkonaqc oli-ikotohom. "Cipotuk muskisqatuwe. Kotama tan tehpu elikit skitap nostomuwon."

"No," Cihkonaqc yawns. "Perhaps he is speaking musikisq (sky language). No ordinary man can understand it."

Neke Koluskap itom, "Wawonol weskuhutokil. Itom, Wa, wa. Nit nit mec wawon Peskotomuhkatiyik eliwihtomuhtit."

At that time Koluskap says, "He is talking about eggs. He's saying, wa, wa. That's what the Passamaquoddy still call an egg—wawon."

Cihkonaqc 'titomon, "Tan-olu eyik?"

Cihkonaqc says, "But where are they?"

Koluskap 'tolokiman walkalin tupqanok. Kehceyawikil moskomonol. Komac Cihkonaqc ulinomonol naka 'tassokinomon.

Koluskap instructs him to dig in the sand. He finds many of them. Cihkonaqc likes the way they look and is awed by them.

Mec-ote toke pemkiskahk cihkonaqcok ponatomuk tupqanok. Nit nit Koluskap eli-pahpiyatpon.

Still, even to this day, turtles lay eggs in the sand. This is how Koluskap jested.

Koluskap Nekotok Skitkomiq

When Koluskap Left the Earth

Neke Koluskap nekotok skitkomiq, nokkahpawolasoponihi cipinaqsultilicihi msi-wenihi. Kiwahqiyik kete, kotama aqamok yali-pisuwapasiwiyik kcihkuk. Kollu-na kotama apc kisi-piskapotasuhkew tan etuci-sipelehlat wonoski. Kci-mochant Cinu kotama apc mahawi pomawsuwinu lahtoqehsonuk. Kotama mecikicik weyossisok, wahantuwok, naka kci-athusossuwok toli-mskuwawiyik tan qihiw eyultihtit pomawsuwinuwok.

At the time when Koluskap left the earth, he had scared away all the evil-looking creatures. Giants, for instance, no longer wandered aimlessly in the forests. Kollu never again could bring darkness by spreading his wings. The great devil Cinu never again devoured people in the north. No evil beasts, devils, or great serpents could be found near where men live.

Nit nekka-macehtuhut mocahantuwok, on Koluskap 'toqetokehkiman skicinu tan aqamok 'toli-kisi-woli-pomasultilin. Kotama-olu 'kisi-wolasuwiyawi. Komac utomitahasikhawal Koluskapiyil, malom-ote kotama 'kisi-wiciyemawi. Etuci-wiqhopaluwat sopayakom Minaskik. Msi-te skicinuwok naka weyossisok 'toliyaniya.

Once all the evil devils have been driven away, Koluskap tries to teach the people how they can live better lives. But he cannot please them. They cause him great worry; finally, he can stay among them no longer. And so he gathers them for a feast along the shore at Minas Basin. All the people and animals attend.

Mehtonukahk, 'tepessin kci-oqitonuk. Skicinuwok 'topinuwaniya tokkiw-ote ehqi-nomiyahtit. Keskayapomahtit, mec-ote-olu nutuwawal elomintulicil. Ahaciw olomi-nawtaqsu elomi-pihcek. Kospon-ote skat nutuwahtihq. Nit-te sonuciw msiw etoli-ciphucultihtit.

At the end of the feast, he climbs into a great canoe. The people watch him until they can no longer see him. When they have lost sight of him, they still hear him singing on his way. His voice gets fainter and fainter as the distance increases. At last they do not hear him at all. There by the water's edge they all stand in a frightened posture.

Naka 'tassokelomoqaniya: weyossisok, mecimiw 'sotawotultusoponik; pesqon 'tolatuwewakonuwa. Sesolahki-ote kotama 'sotawotultiwiyik. Etuci-wiwonaspayultihtit. Nit tan-ote wen eli-wewiphuwet: yat-te nekom pesq oloqiye, apc kotok tetta. Kotama apc mawiyewiyik apc-oc yaka Koluskap apattehkuwat. Apc-oc mawona, on-oc apc skicinuwok 'sankewi-mawiyaniya. Tokec-olu msi-te keq 'kiwacehtun.

And then something strange happens to them: creatures once understood one another—they had one common language. All of a sudden, they do not understand one another. They are so frightened they go crazy with fear. Then each one runs off on his own; that one goes one way and another that way. They will not gather again until Koluskap returns to them. He will bring them together again, and then the people will assemble peacefully. But now, he makes everything feel lonely.

Itasu, neke Koluskap nekolat skicinu, wapi-kuhkukhahs oloqiyess etoli-mocimkahqihkek. Kat-tehc-ona apc apaciyew, tokkiw yakahc naci-wolasikotuwat Koluskapiyil. Nit-te mec toke, yali-motehtaqsu lamahqihkuk. Itom, "Kuhkuhu." Koluskap 'toqimum, 'kotunkewku, wiwonasi-pomituwiyawolotuwok msi-te noluwiw skitkomiq. 'Sesomi-qiluwahawal 'tutemkuwal. Cipokihtaqsuwok etolewehtuhtit.

It is said that when Koluskap left the people, the white owl went into the thick woods. And he will not return again until the day that he goes to greet Koluskap. There, even now, he can be heard deep in the forest. He says, "Kuhkuhu." Koluskap's loons, his hunters, fly aimlessly all over the earth. They cannot find their master. Loudly they howl.

Mesq neke macahahq kakehsikoton, 'tahkinuwehtuwasoponihi 'toqimum. 'Tiyaponihi, "Tan-oc wot wen qiluwihit, pesqonc tan wen eli-pawatok ntoli-milan pskuwit, tan tehpu keq. Kehtol kahk siki-qecehtasu, pihcetu komac. Niktok-oc siki-mihkuhkomacik tan yukt eqeci-mskuwicik."

Many years before he left, he had given his loons a message. He had told them, "Whoever seeks me, I shall give one thing that he wants when he finds me, whatever it may be. Of course, it will be hard going and very difficult to try, for the distance is very long. Those who try to find me will be ones who endure great hardship and suffering."

Itasu, nuhuwok skicinuwok 'kisi-qecehtuniya, pesq Wolastoq naka nisuwok Panuwapskewiyik.

It is said that three men made the attempt, one Maliseet and two Penobscots.

Oluwikonok kehsikoton pomkenuwok, on yaka keka 'pecuhsamaniya. Komac sikikon pemkomuhtit elkepolasik, naka komac usikonomahtiniya. Pcossol nuhuwok kisuhsok etutok wikilit, kis nutomuwaniya metekilelicihi 'temis. Elomite wecuwawkomuwahtit 'sakomamuwal wik, ahaciw olomi-kintaqsu 'temis. Malom-ote moskuwawal 'kihci-sakomamuwal, not msiw sakomawamat skitapiyi naka weyossis. Wolitahasuwi-nomiyukuwal naka waniyukuniya. 'toqecimulkuniya keq oli-pawatomuk.

They travel for seven years, and they at last almost reach him. Making their way along the trail is very difficult, and they encounter many hardships. Although they are still three months' journey from where he lives, they can already hear his dogs barking. The closer they get to their chief's house, the louder his dogs bark. At last they find their great chief, the one who governs all men and animals. He is very glad to see them, and he entertains them warmly. He asks them what it is they wish to have.

Pesq, kehci-skicinuwit, li-pawatom nihtawi-kotunkan. Sapiku, kenoq-olu nutatahamqosu pomawsuwinuwihkuk, ipocol kotama ntawi-kotunkew. Nit 'toli-wihkutomon nihtawi-msonan naka nehpahan weyossis. Nit Koluskap milan pipiqatossis: motewolonuwi-pipiqat. Msi-tehc wen nutok, wolsotomon. Lahsonuwiw, tan tehpu weyossisol nuhsuhkakulc tan wen putuwatok.

One, the oldest man, wants to know how to hunt. He looks trustworthy, but he is not respected among the people because he does not know how to hunt. He asks to be able to catch and kill animals. So Koluskap gives him a little whistle—a whistle with special powers. Everyone that hears it will like its sound. It has such power that any animal will follow the person who blows it.

Nisewey skicin yaha, "Keq-op-olu wikitahatomon?"

The second man is asked, "What is it that you desire?"

"Nmuhsalkun ehpicik."

"That women be fond of me."

Koluskap 'tiyal, "Kehsuwok?"

Koluskap says "How many?"

“Kotama-te kinuweluwiyik, tehpu tepeluhtic.”

“It doesn’t have to be a lot, just let there be enough.”

Nit nutuwat Koluskap, katekon wolitahatomuwon, kenoq-olu wolomuwiqetutom. Milan ptoqap, sakoli-kpopite. ’Tiyal, “Musa apqopituhkoc yaka kikok peciyayin.” Wolasuweltomon nisewey skicin naka macahan.

When Koluskap hears him, he doesn’t approve of the idea; nevertheless, he smiles warmly. He gives him a bag, tightly tied. He says to him, “Don’t untie the bag until you get to your house.” The second man gives thanks, and then departs.

Nuhuwewey skinuhs, komac wolapewiw, tehpu-tahk eli-wahkathomat. Tehpu moshun oltokte tan ’toli-kisi-mskomon weci-kisi-siktelomuwat skicinu.

The third young man is quite handsome, but he has very little common sense. His heart is set on nothing but finding a way to make the people laugh.

Qecimula, “Keq-olu kil pawatomon?”

He is asked, “And what is it you want?”

’Titomon, “Komac op nulasuwiyukun kisi-mskomon tan ntoli-kisi-assoktaqsin weci-kisehtuwuk skicinuwok ’siktelomultiniya.”

He says, “It would please me very much if you could find a way for me to make an odd noise, so that I can make the people laugh.”

Nit wihkutok assoktaqsuwik, awisiw nutasu Waponahkik. Tehpu toli-nutasu wahkehsonul ucikansonul memhuwi-sehtayiw kci-kcihkuk. Mec-ote-ona iyu wahkehsu siki-motewolon kosona assokapiyit skitap kecicihtaq tan oli-peciptasu. Etuci-assoktaqahk, tan yukt nutokik metesuwwewik, cuwi-siktelomultuwok.

The strange noise he asks for is rarely heard in Wabanaki territory. It can be heard only in a few huts far back in the great forest. There are still a few fearsome motewolons, or men with extraordinary powers, who how it is produced. It sounds so odd that those who hear it resounding have to laugh.

Nit Koluskap 'tolokiman Nimaqsuwehsuwol kcihkuk naci-kotunotulin keqsi-wecopahkik. Nit micasik, assokkahsuwiw tahalu nit skinuhs eli-pawatok. Oli-kinuwehtuwa kotama 'samehtuwon tokkiw yaka wikok peciyat. Nit-olu samehtaq, kat-tehc woliyukuwon. Wolasuweltomon skinuhs, naka uci-macahan.

So Koluskap sends Nimaqsuwehs, the sable, into the woods to go pick a certain kind of root. When eaten, it will bring the strange effects that the boy wants. He is instructed not to touch it until he arrives at his house. If he touches it, it will not have a good effect on him. The young man gives thanks and departs.

Oluwikonok kehsikoton 'qonkomoniya apaciw. Pcossol tehpu oluwikonok kehsukoniw pawalqahk, wesuwemahahtit elkepolasik. On yat-te wen 'toloqiyan 'tutenek. Pesq tehpu apaciyat wikok apc: wot nit kotunkewin. Pipiqatossis 'pitsonakonok ehtek, kat-te keq 'tomitahatomu. Yaluhse kcihkuk. Tan qenawsit, mecimi-tehc mossihtun pehqey wikok.

It takes them seven years to make the return journey. Only seven days' journey is required when they make their way to the main path. Then each one goes toward his own village. Only one makes it back to his house—this is the hunter. With his little whistle in his pocket, he has no worries. He walks about in the woods. As long as he lives, he will always have a good supply of fresh meat in his house.

Not pawatokoss muhsalkun ehpilicihi, muck-ote kotama mosonawon nisuwihticil. Kotama pihcetu luhsew, tuciw apqopitaq motqap. Sakhintuhtihtit welikulticik pilsqehsok, olikultuwok tahalutehp wapi-polesok. Wiwonahsikotaku. Ksihposiyalokiqawolotuwok naka sisselamsuwiw 'piyehsumuwal. Wiwonasihpusultuwok. Yut ehkosqenahtit, ayut wecemahtit. Ahaciw olomi-wiwonasihpusultuwok. Alu mimiwehla, kotama tahk ciksotomuhtiwiyik. 'toqeci-mskomin, kotama tahk. Etoli-aluwolatok, wehqalamuhsuke. Malom-ote mehciniya. Yuktok pemi-tutapasicik moskuwawal, cel kis citoniye. Tan-olu 'tolitpiyaniya pilsqehsok, kotama-te kcicihqotu.

That one who wanted to be loved by women, he doesn't even get a wife. He does not walk far before he unties his bag. Beautiful maidens come forth singing; they look like white doves. They surround him. Their eyes burn with desire and their hair blows about in the wind. They become wild. They hug him and kiss him. They become more and more uncontrollable. Even though he sends them away, they do not listen. He tries to escape, but he cannot. He gasps for air, suffocating. At last he dies. Those walking by find him, and he is already stiff. What happened to the maidens is not known.

Nuhuwewey skicin elomiyat 'qotuhkayiw. Wolitahasu. Sesolahki-te mihqitahatomon eli keq Koluskap kisi-milatpon. Kat-te mace-tpitahatomuwon yuhutpon: "Peciyayin kikok yaka kmicin." Nit-olu woliw muskehtun wecopahkik. Woli-te-na micin.

The third man goes off by himself. He is happy. All of a sudden he remembers that Koluskap has given him something. He does not even begin to think about what he was told: "When you get to your house, then you eat it." But right away he takes out the root. And then and there he eats it.

Cel mesq nokkahtuwon, nit etuci-wewitahatok eli nekomc kisi-assoktaqsit: 'petkakun elsonuwik motewolonuwi-wecopahkik milutpon. Memhuwihtaqot. Pahpuwi-wahantuwok te 'kisokehkoluhtomoniya elomi-pokotahqewiyak elomotonihkek, elomi-cinkomikek, ayut walcokekil. Malom-ote tihtokol 'tasitemal. Komac palitahamsu, naci-yali-paluhsan, 'putuwan. Wehqapuhset-ote, wolitahasu, tahalu-te sipsis. Kenoq-olu nanakiw, solahkiw peci-naskatahamsu. Nemiyat otuhkol, napicehtun pahq. Mace-kikimskuwan. Nahaht-ote keti-motkiyaqhomat, kotama-te 'kisi-kolonomuwon motewolonuwi-assoktaqsuwakon milutpon. Ansa-te mocahantuwihtaqsu. Otuhk olomotqahwa. Nit skinuhs etuci-nipskatuwet.

Before he has finished it, he remembers that he will be able to make the strange noise: the strength of the magic root that he was given comes upon him. It makes a loud noise. The jesting devils are able to imitate it as it echoes from the high mountains, from the lowlands, and from the swamps. Eventually, the screech-owl answers him. He feels so proud, he struts along blowing. As he walks along, he is as happy as a little bird. After a while, however, he begins to feel uncomfortable. When he sees a deer, he puts an arrow on the string. He began to stalk it. Just when he raises his bow to aim, he can no longer hold the magical wonder-noise he was given. He really makes an evil sound. The deer jumps away. Then the young man curses.

Peciyat Panuwapskek, epahsi-siktelamu. 'sami-ktomakapewiw wihqinuwan. Niktok-olu nihkani-skicinuwok, sapi-pahpulticik amsqahs. Siktiyelomultuwok. Nit kekesk skinuhs wolitahaskakun. Nit-olu elomi-kehsukoniwik ahaci-te 'tolomi-naskatahamawal, nit-te na nekom 'siwawsin. Macahan kcihkuk naci-nehpuhusin. Nit-te na Cipelahq 'pakskalituwiyan 'ciw aluhkihkuk naka macephan lamkik. Nit miluts assoktaqsuwakon, kiseltomuwan 'tuwehkan etoli-piskahtek. Kotama-te apc tama toli-nutaqsiw skitapewihkuk.

When he arrives at Penobscot, he is half-starved. He is too pitiful-looking to arouse laughter. Those elders are moved to laughter at first. They laugh hard. This makes the young man feel a little happier. But as the days go on, they think less and less of him, and he himself grows tired of living. He goes away into the woods to kill himself. Then Cipelahq swoops down from the clouds and takes him to the lower world. The wondrous noise that was given to him, he is allowed to use in the dark world. He is never again heard among men.

Mettokot yut acomuwakon.

This story is ended.

GLOSSARY OF UNFAMILIAR PASSAMAQUODDY WORDS IN THE KOLUSKAP STORIES

OLD WORD	EQUIVALENT TERM	MEANING
altestakonok	piwsoqewi-walotek	on a wooden gaming dish
apattehkuwat	apaciyat	when he comes back
apoqahk	kahpotayahk	throw him off
cikonaqstek	citoneyu	stiff
’cocokayessin	nahtokahtehsin	goes ashore
eli-kecalokiqat	wiwoniw ’sisqihkuk	around his eyes
eli-koskitomek	eli-spitomek	where it is deep
eli-pitpek	eli-pihtewiyak	where the water is foamy
eli-seksultilit	eli-siktehpayultilit	how afraid they are
elkepolasik	awtossis, awtossisok	path
elomi-pusilicil	elomi-sukilicil	as he is pushing off, paddling
epahsakom	milawiw	away from shore into the water
etoli-kposki-nasqahahtit	etoli-nasqahahtit tokkiw kewilit	they are combing him until he falls asleep
etoli-mocimkahqihkek	elomi-sikipisokek	into thick woods
etoloqassihtit	etoli-nahtokahahtit	where they go ashore
etuci-paqtek	etuci-sakolocokuhsewik	it is so thick
etuci-wiqhopaluwat	etuci-wihqimat pomawsuwinu	invites people to a feast
kehci-wewisilicil	kci-wewisol	busybody
keqoss wapolessu	keq leyu	something is wrong
keti-motkiyaqhomat	keti-ewepi-wolaqhomat	when he lifts weapon to aim

GLOSSARY (continued)

OLD WORD	EQUIVALENT TERM	MEANING
’ketoloqtahan	’tuwalokihtahan kosona ’paskoloqihtahan	chops hole in the ice
kisaposiyusiyin	kisi-wicukemsiyin	be able to help yourself
’kisi-’tahapiyatomuwon	’kisi-ksomikomuwon kosona ’kisi-nihkanikomuwon	cannot manage boat
kisi-tehc yali-topskans	kisi-tehc yaliqaha	you will be able to roll around
kiwahq	natomokilok kci-pomawsuwin, skitkomiqewi-mocahant	evil giant
kmottokassiw	knahtokassiw	you [will not] go ashore
kmottokhomupon	knahtokahomupon	we go ashore
knaci-monawonapon	knaci-qiluwahtunennul wawonol	we go gather eggs
knacitahamkuk	kmusqitahamkuk	they hate you, are out to get you
kospon-ote	mam-ote	finally
kpiscopolan	kcuwahpahkan	throw him into the water [to drown]
kpiscopolokun	kcuwahpahkalkun	they throw you into the water [to drown]
ksilhuss	knisuwiyeq mihtaqsol	your father-in-law
kuwahsonuk	tehsahqiw oposik mace-suhkolihkat	on a rotting log
lahtoqehsonuk	punkik	north
Laks	skicinuwi-wahant	“Indian Devil” [possibly wolverine]
lamahqihkuk	lamiw kcihkuk	in the woods

mace-menakatkeniniya	mace-menakaciyaniya	they begin to go slowly
macilqenuwit	macehlat wonoski	move his wings
maciyehlukultiniya	maceqahtuhukhotiniya	they float away
malom-ote	mam-ote	finally
mehtaluktek	etoli-mettek aluhkol	where the clouds end
metesuwwewik	metehtaqahk	it is heard echoing
mimiwehla	macehtaha	he sends them away, chases them away
mokoses	peyaqotek opos	soot, burnt wood residue
monomeqakon	elahtuwessihtit petakiyik	lightning
moqtuniyaqhan	’tapqotekomuwan ’tunuwal ewehket oposisol	he props their mouths open with a stick
mottokhomoniya	nahtokahomoniya	they go ashore
msi / msi-te / msiw	psi / psi-te / psiw	all, every
muhsalkun	’kosi-iyakun	they love him, are very fond of him
mulahkek pemahqihkek	kcihqi-lamiw	deep in the woods
musikisqatuwe	’kansuhswi-skicinuwatuwe	he speaks “sky-language”
naci-koluluwewan	nathomahsuwewan	he goes to speak on his behalf
nacitahamtihticil	musqitahamtihticil	his enemy
nakahkalsu	nakayahkalsu	he goes slowly (on purpose)
naksqiyik	pilsqehsisok mesq nipuwultihtihq	unmarried young women
nanakiw	mahkiyewossis	in a little while
natomokil	kinkil	he is big
neqtelakutulticik	ehpit, skitap, naka nicanuwa mawi-wikulticik	family
nika	nikuwoss	my mother

GLOSSARY (continued)

OLD WORD	EQUIVALENT TERM	MEANING
nimiyanol	macephal	he takes it along
nmuhsacin	nkosi-iywa	I love him, am fond of him
nmuhsalkun	nkosi-iyakun	they love me, are very fond of me
ntuwasom	ntuwasisom	my child
nucikansonnuk	nikononnuk	in our houses
oposiyahqem	oposi-tomhikon	wooden club
pahpultin	layyawolotin	playing
’pakskalituwiyan	’sesolahki-cinituwiyan	he swoops down suddenly
peci ma seskimiyawomolsiw	peci-ksinuhka	he feels sickness coming on
peci-wehse	petolamson	the wind comes up
’pehenomum	mossis	his sisters
’pehenomumuwal	mossisuwal	their sister
pehqey	wiyuhs	fresh meat
pemikhoticik	wikulticik	those who dwell there
pemotonihkek	espahkek ktahkomiq	on high ground
petson	petolamson	the wind comes up
piqekit	elomalokosit	hollow
’piscopolaniya	’cuwahpahkalaniya	they throw him into the water [to drown]
pitpewiyak	pihtewiyak	where the water is foamy
polesok	sipsok	doves
ponapsqahson	ponapsqewi-’tomakon	stone pipe (for smoking)
’posqentun	macentun	he bursts into song

puskiw	kakehs	often, many times
puskosonessihq	puspelihq makson	he [does not] get his shoes wet
qesimuhtuwak	kalsuwamak	you hide from them, escape from them
'qesqicituwiyan	pasicituwiyat	he flies over
sapiku	wolomahtu	he is of good character
seksihkoc	siktehpayihkoc	don't be afraid
'seksin	'siktehpayin	she is afraid
seksultin	siktehpayultin	being afraid
'siktiyaqosan	'tolaqosan tokkiw mehcinelit	he burns him to death
sipuwahkuk	sonuciw sipuk	on the river bank
'siwiyi	elakumacihi	his relatives
skinuhsuwok	skinuhsisok	young men
'tapotukonapinol	'tapotehsinnol	he leans on it
'tatiyuhewikotuwan	'tiyan, "apcoc knomiyul[pa]"	he bids him [them] farewell
teponaskuhyak	elomiyak	after a time
'tolakonis	kcihqewin ewehkahat keti-kipehlat oposiyil kosona stahqonul	wedge
'toli-tpahmuwal	'tiyal	he tells him, promises him
'toqetpehkuwan	'toqeci-tehsahqikapuwin	he tries to stand on him
'tosalawal	'sehtanehsewatomoniya	they inhale it
tukcokiyak	pihtewiyak	it is thick with foam
uci-pusultiniya	uci-macahawolotiniya	they depart in a canoe
ucikansonul	skicinuwi-wikuwamol	old dwellings
wahkehs elinehsemok	mahiyewossis	in a short time, in a few breaths

GLOSSARY (continued)

OLD WORD	EQUIVALENT TERM	MEANING
wapap	skicinuwi kospisun kosona psihkusunol kehcitomawotik	wampum
wapsqewiyil	wapeyuwi-muwinewi-motekon	white bearskin
wecopahkik	wocopskeweyal	roots
wehqalamuhsuke	koskotunuhuke	he chokes [suffocating]
wehqapskelute	psoni-pkotete lamikuwam	it fills up inside with smoke
welkomawik	tepi-wolinaqahk	good enough in appearance
wesiwesticik	nisuwok siwehsok	two brothers
wesuwemahahtit	petapasihtit	they return on foot
wihqihtahtetul	’catokiwol	they are shriveled
wocuk	espahkek ktahkomiq	on a mountain
wolasuwewi-siktelomultiniya	’siktelomuhtawotultiniya	they smile affectionately [at one another]
woli-ehpicik	pilkatomuhticik ehpicik	good women; newly married women

PRONOUNCING PASSAMAQUODDY

VOWELS – *A, E, I, O, U*

Letter	English	Passamaquoddy	Translation
a	father	ahahs	'horse'
e	bed	epit	'sitting'
eh	tack	*eh*pit	'woman'
i	mach*i*ne	*i*pis	'whip'
o	apron	*o*pos	'tree, stick'
u	dune	*u*ten	'town'
aw	how	a*w*t	'road'
ew	*Europa* (*Spanish*)	n*ew*	'four'
iw	f*ew*	lam*iw*	'within'
ay	p*ie*	sep*ay*	'this morning'
ey	gr*ey*	piks*ey*	'pork'

CONSONANTS

The letters *h*, *l*, *m*, *n*, *w*, and *y* represent sounds much the same as those in English; *h* is pronounced before a vowel, silent or lightly pronounced before a consonant. The letters *c*, *k*, *p*, *q*, *s*, and *t* have a sound that depends on whether the letter occurs next to another consonant, as shown in the chart below.

Passamaquoddy Letter	When next to another consonant (except the personal prefix n- 'I, we,') or next to an apostrophe, sounds like English...	When not next to a consonant or apostrophe, or when following the personal prefix n- 'I, we,' sounds like English...
c	ch	j
k	k	g
p	p	b
q	kw	gw
s	s	z
t	t	d

BIOGRAPHIES

WAYNE A. NEWELL grew up at Sipayik with Passamaquoddy as his first language. He has been active for more than 50 years in promoting and revitalizing the Passamaquoddy language. He created and directed the first Native bilingual education program at Motahkomikuk in the 1970s, and has also served the community as health director, member of the tribal council, and president for 27 years of the tribe's Northeast Blueberry Company. He holds an honorary doctorate from the University of Southern Maine. Newell is the first Native person to be appointed to the University of Maine Board of Trustees, and was also appointed by presidents Carter and Obama to serve as a member of the National Advisory Council on Indian Education. He lives at Motahkomikuk with his wife Sandra, four children, and many grandchildren and great-grandchildren.

ROBERT M. LEAVITT has worked with Passamaquoddy language speakers since 1971, first in the Maine communities and later as professor of education at the University of New Brunswick, where he was appointed professor emeritus upon retirement. He developed curriculum and materials for the Passamaquoddy bilingual education program at Motahkomikuk in the 1970s and went on to co-author the Passamaquoddy-Maliseet Dictionary with David A. Francis, of Sipayik. The dictionary continues to grow and develop online, at pmportal.org. Leavitt lives in Dufferin Parish, near St. Stephen, New Brunswick.

NEWELL AND LEAVITT first met in 1971, as graduate students at Harvard University, and they have worked together since then on Passamaquoddy language projects, writing, editing, translating, recording, and teaching.

www.ingramcontent.com/pod-product-compliance
Lightning Source LLC
Chambersburg PA
CBHW082106090726
47910CB00009B/2606

9780998819570